GUIDE TO LANDSCAPE AND LAWN CARE

McGraw-Hill Paperbacks
Home Improvement Series

Guide to Plumbing

Guide to Electrical Installation and Repair

Guide to Roof and Gutter Installation and Repair

Guide to Wallpaper and Paint

Guide to Paneling and Wallboard

Guide to Landscape and Lawn Care

Guide to Brick, Concrete, and Stonework

Guide to Carpentry

Guide to Furniture Refinishing and Antiquing

Guide to Bathroom and Kitchen Remodeling

GUIDE TO LANDSCAPE AND LAWN CARE

McGRAW-HILL BOOK COMPANY

New York   St. Louis   San Francisco   Auckland   Bogotá   Düsseldorf
Johannesburg   London   Madrid   Mexico   Montreal   New Delhi   Panama
Paris   São Paulo   Singapore   Sydney   Tokyo   Toronto

1 2 3 4 5 6 7 8 9 0 SMSM 8 3 2 1 0

Library of Congress Cataloging in Publication Data

Main entry under title:

Guide to landscape and lawn care.

  (McGraw-Hill paperbacks home improvement series)
  Originally published in 1975 by Minnesota Mining and Manufacturing
Company, Automotive-Hardware Trades Division, St. Paul, in the home
pro guide series, under title: The home pro landscape and lawn care guide.
  1. Landscape gardening. 2. Lawns. I. Minnesota Mining and
Manufacturing Company. Automotive-Hardware Trades Division. Home
pro landscape and lawn care guide.
SB473.G85 1980 635.9'64 79-27037
ISBN 0-07-045972-X

Cover photo: Costa Manos/Magnum Photos

Contents

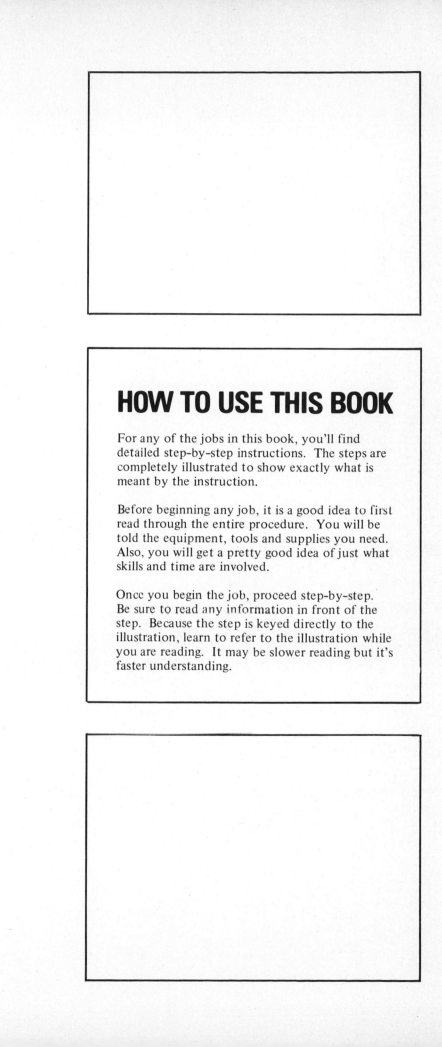

HOW TO USE THIS BOOK

For any of the jobs in this book, you'll find detailed step-by-step instructions. The steps are completely illustrated to show exactly what is meant by the instruction.

Before beginning any job, it is a good idea to first read through the entire procedure. You will be told the equipment, tools and supplies you need. Also, you will get a pretty good idea of just what skills and time are involved.

Once you begin the job, proceed step-by-step. Be sure to read any information in front of the step. Because the step is keyed directly to the illustration, learn to refer to the illustration while you are reading. It may be slower reading but it's faster understanding.

GUIDE TO LANDSCAPE AND LAWN CARE

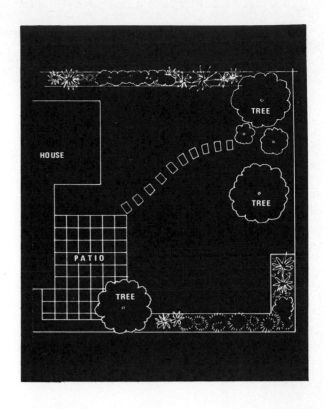

LANDSCAPING

The dual goal in planning landscaping is to design a pleasant environment for your family, and at the same time to design features that are usable, long lasting and easy to live with. This section of the book discusses the overall planning of a yard and ways to achieve the desired results. The sections of the book that follow provide detailed recommendations for designing landscaping features.

Begin the overall planning of your yard by taking a walk around your home and yard with a pencil in hand. Take an inventory of what you have, what you would like to keep, what you would like to add and perhaps, what you would like to eliminate. The same approach can be used for planning a new yard or remodeling an old yard.

To increase the probability of having attractive features in your landscaping plan, consider the following criteria during the tour of your yard.

- The house should have an inviting or interesting look as you approach the entrance from the street or driveway.

- The yard should blend naturally with adjacent property, not contrast with it.

- The buildings in the yard should be framed with trees and plantings to create a natural setting.

BEFORE

AFTER

- If there is a pleasant view from the house or yard, plan to preserve the scene. Conversely, if all you see are rooftops and garages, the scene may be screened or blocked out.
- On flat suburban lots without noteworthy natural features, you may want to create some. Garden pools, fountains, arbors, rock gardens, or fireplaces are examples. These features are most effective when they can also be viewed from inside the home.
- Slopes in the natural setting can be terraced to make the yard more interesting. Steep slopes should be planted to prevent erosion. Walkways on slopes must be properly graded to prevent slipping and falling.

You will want to design features into your landscaping plan that will make your home more usable and easier to live with. Take the following criteria into account as you tour your home and yard.

All family members must be considered. Small children need a play area. Older children may need areas for sports or hobbies. Adults may want a quiet retreat, a gardening area, or a place for outdoor entertaining.

An outdoor living area is usually desirable. Some outdoor living areas are not used because they are not easily accessible from the living areas of the house. Making a door out of a window or building a pathway to the area are two ways of correcting this situation.

The yard should contain provisions for clothes drying, storing trash cans, garden equipment, bicycles, boats, etc. Service areas should be screened from the other areas of the yard or house, and easily accessible from the kitchen or garage.

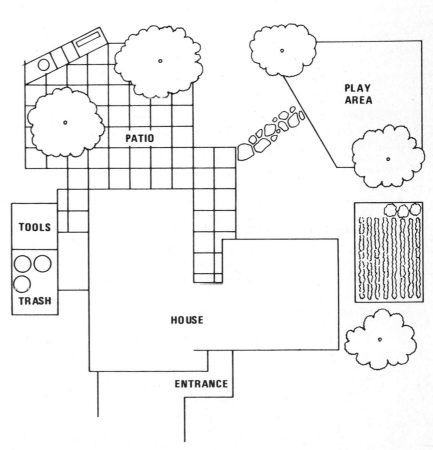

Plan your landscaping to make the most of the climate you live in.

- Note the sun patterns on your property and determine where you might want to create shade for outdoor living. This can be done by constructing a patio roof, with vines growing over lathing, or by planting trees. Don't forget to consider shading children's play areas.

- Note the prevailing wind pattern. Outdoor areas may become usable for more months of the year if strong winds are diverted. This can be accomplished by using fencing or plants as a windbreak.

- If insects are a problem in your area, consider screening in the patio.

- Check the property to see where water flows off the house roof after heavy rains and if it is carried away properly. Note whether water stands in spots for a long time before it evaporates.

There are many more features to consider when you plan your landscaping. They affect the ultimate appearance of your property and how pleasant it will be to use. Some typical features are discussed below to emphasize the need for and possible benefits from careful planning.

- Portions of front yards can be reclaimed for private use by installing a screen or hedge. This is especially helpful if the house is set far back on the lot. Keep in mind any setback regulations in your area.

- Small lots, with shallow back yards, seem larger if patios or pathways lead the eye around the corner of the house. Another trick is to create "hidden" areas with a small fence.

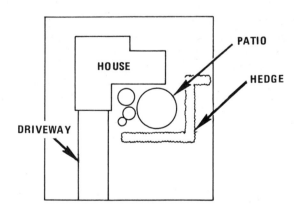

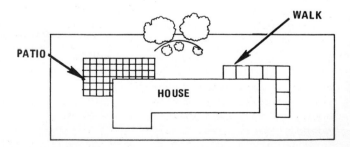

- The time of year may influence landscaping work. Wet or very cold weather can hamper construction efforts. Planting times vary for different plants.

- Consider the ages of the family members. Play areas for small children should be planned so they can be used for other activities as the children grow older and their interests change. For example, a sandbox near a terrace can be converted into a spot for plants or a rose garden.

- Be sure a desired area will be used for enough years to make the cost worthwhile. A paved basketball court may lie idle after the first few years.

- Many a plan has gone wrong when an owner discovers how much work is necessary to keep up the yard. Maintenance can be reduced by avoiding large expanses of lawn. If you do not need a large lawn area, select ground cover or other plants that do not need continual trimming or cutting. Paving, broken up with small areas of plants, is another way to reduce lawn area.

- Making an overall plan that identifies all of the paving or the carpentry needs, so that they can be accomplished at one time, will save money. You may also get discounts by buying all of your plants at one time.

- It may pay to hire a professional to do complicated grading or things you may not feel confident about handling yourself. Errors require the cost of correction. If you want to try your hand at construction, such as pouring concrete, test your skill on a small project like a few stepping stones.

- Smaller and cheaper isn't necessarily better if the area isn't used.

- The biggest savings in cost come through proper planning. Planning shouldn't be done in a hurry. Proper planning may require that several weekends be spent looking through literature, looking at other yards and public gardens, drawing up the plan, and then giving it a trial test.

After you assemble your ideas for what you would like in your yard, make a detailed plan that brings it all together.

It will be worthwhile to make a scale drawing of your property on graph paper. Figure out a workable scale, such as 10 feet to the inch. In your drawing, locate the house, garage, or any other structures, and existing trees or shrubs you want to keep. Indicate the driveway, sidewalks or fences you have. Show by symbol the doors and windows. Note the height from the ground to the bottoms of the windows. Show the location of the rooms within the house to help you effectively place any outdoor living and service areas. Walk through the house, look out the windows, and note on the drawing where you would like to create a pleasing view. Locate underground utility and sewer or septic tank lines. Any pavement additions must be planned to allow future access to these lines.

Use tracing paper over your scale drawings of the yard and work out several alternate plans for landscaping the yard. Experiment with different geometric shapes that define areas. Squares or rectangles are the easiest for most people to work with. You could also use circles or ovals.

Curves are generally the hardest to design. Unless you are very artistic, use whatever shape you choose throughout your design. An exception might be a curved flower border along a long fence.

Typical proposed landscaping designs make use of squares [1], circles [2], and rectangles [3].

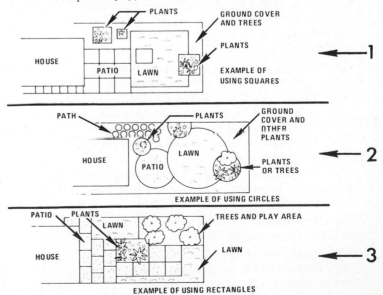

EXAMPLE OF USING SQUARES

EXAMPLE OF USING CIRCLES

EXAMPLE OF USING RECTANGLES

Size is an important factor when planning areas for specific purposes.

- Walkways, gates and entrances should be wide enough to accommodate patio furniture, boats, etc., as needed by the owner.

- Terraces should be ample and not as small as indoor rooms. Out of doors, people like to stretch out.

- Driveways, especially double driveways, should allow room to step out on the driveway surface instead of the lawn and to open car doors.

- When placing paved terraces under trees, allow an open area equal to the drip line around the tree. The open area can become an effective planting bed.

The suggestions below will help you "test" out your plan before you start any construction. You will need long and short stakes and lots of string.

The tall stakes connected by strings can outline decorative screens, fences or hedges. Short stakes and strings can outline raised planter beds, or terracing of slopes. A long length of rope or a hose can outline flower beds or planting borders that adjoin the lawn. Terraces or patios can be outlined by sprinkling sand at the outside edge of the desired area. Use stakes to mark placement of large trees.

Now you can walk around your yard to check traffic patterns and to determine whether the proposed features are attractive and usable.

Size can be tested by placing card tables and chairs on patios. Sit at the table. Walk around while the chairs are pulled out to see if there is room to move easily.

You can place lawn mowers, wheelbarrows, etc. in the space provided for storage to see if there is enough room.

Have the children ride bicycles and run around in the areas designated for them.

Leave your "temporary" landscaping in place for a week or two to confirm that it is what you had in mind.

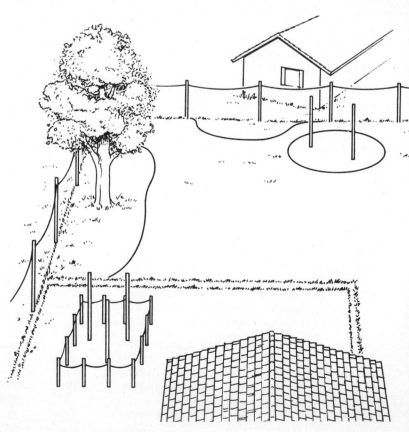

Sometimes the terrain must be corrected before landscaping can begin. This is extremely difficult, if not impossible, to do after fences or pavements are added.

Complex grading situations where there are steep slopes or water draining from someone else's property to yours and then off yours to another piece of property should be handled by a professional. If you have doubts about how difficult the grading problem might be, your local city or county engineer can tell you what must be done.

Lawns need a smooth surface that is sloped enough to carry excess water away from the house and then off the property.

Soil should slope away from a house at a rate of 1/4 inch per foot as a minimum. This would amount to 2-1/2 inches at a point 10 feet away from house. The slope can be checked using a string, stakes and a level as shown at the right. Have someone hold the level for you when tying the string to make sure the string is perfectly level.

DISTANCE BETWEEN STRING AND GROUND 10 FT. FROM HOUSE EQUALS 2-1/2 IN.

HOUSE

LEVEL

10'

STRING

SOIL SLOPE

If you are planning to do any cement or brickwork along with your landscaping, be sure to consider the slope of these items, too. For example, patios driveways and sidewalks should be sloped to permit water to run off.

The minimum effective sloping is 1/4 inch per foot. The maximum safe sloping in areas that freeze is 5/8 inches per foot. This drop continues from the center to the outside edges if the patio is located away from the house. For patios next to the house, the slope drops from the house to the outside edges of the paving. Use the method of checking slopes illustrated at the right.

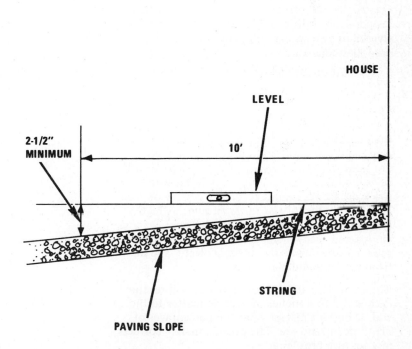

HOUSE

LEVEL

10'

2-1/2" MINIMUM

STRING

PAVING SLOPE

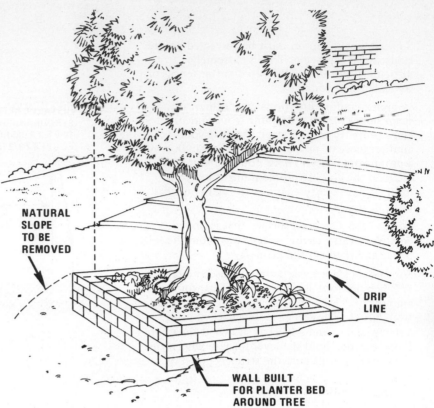

NATURAL
SLOPE
TO BE
REMOVED

DRIP
LINE

WALL BUILT
FOR PLANTER BED
AROUND TREE

If your property has slopes which are steeper than 5/8 inch per foot you should plan to have steps built into walkways that go up the slope. These can be made to be an attractive landscaping feature of your yard.

If you grade around existing trees, the soil level to the drip line must not be disturbed. If you add or remove soil to grade, retain raised planting beds or build walls around existing trees.

SOIL CONDITIONS

Soil conditions determine to a great extent how well things will grow in your yard. There is no better time to correct them than the present. Proper soil conditions will promote healthy growth of everything you plant and simplify yard maintenance.

Soil conditions are made up of three factors:

> Texture
> Nutrients
> Ph factor

A soil texture is determined by the amounts of clay, sand and silt it contains. Sandy soil does not hold water long enough for plants to absorb it. Soil containing too much clay holds water too long. Plants cannot receive necessary oxygen in waterlogged soil and roots may rot. A high percentage of clay allows soil to become compacted easily. This makes it difficult for roots to spread and also prevents water and air from reaching the plant roots.

The corrective action for improving soil texture is to add 2 to 3 inches of organic matter to the soil. It doesn't matter what the percentages of clay, silt or sand are. The organic matter corrects any texture problems.

Organic matter cannot be added later without tearing up the entire lawn or planting area. For this reason, it is recommended that you add organic matter no matter what you think your soil texture might be.

Organic matter is generally available as peat moss, compost, sawdust, or ground corn cobs. Your nursery will tell you what is available in your area.

Organic matter that is added to the soil uses up nitrogen as it decomposes. To compensate for this, add twice the amount of nitrogen when you add the nutrient requirements of the soil.

The pH of the soil is a measure of its acidity (sour) or alkalinity (sweet). A numbered scale has been established for pH factors. The pH factor for a soil is important because a chemical imbalance can prevent nutrients in the soil from being used by plant roots. A very fertile soil will produce thin growth if the soil is too acid or alkaline. Areas of heavy rainfall usually have an acid soil and dry areas an alkaline soil.

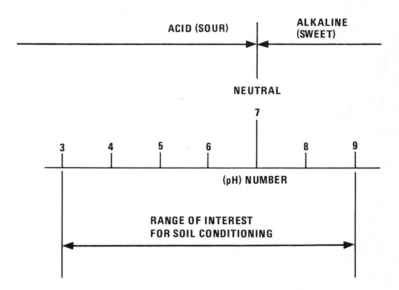

To correct the pH factor of your soil, you must first determine what it is. There are soil testing kits for measuring pH factors at most garden supply stores or nurseries. The kits contain complete instructions and define the neutral range acceptable to most plants. They also contain instructions for applying chemicals to correct the pH (lime for acid soil and sulfur for alkaline soil).

Many soil testing kits also provide for determining any nutrient deficiency which may exist in the soil. For healthy growth, plants require nitrogen, phosphorus and potassium. In some areas of the dry West, there is also an iron deficiency in the soil. The test kits do not usually include provisions for testing for iron. You can check with your local nursery to see if iron is required in your area. Instructions with the kits cover testing and the proper fertilizers to correct nutrient deficiencies.

If test kits are not available for testing nutrient deficiency, use a fertilizer high in nitrogen for lawn areas and high in phosphorus for ground cover and other plants.

Fertilizers come with numbered formulas, such as 10-6-4. The first number is the percentage of nitrogen per 100 pounds; the second, phosphorus; and the third, potassium. Amounts to use are on the package.

Remember to double the amount of nitrogen to compensate for the addition of organic matter. This still holds true when you use a test kit or follow fertilizer package recommendations.

All of the ingredients necessary to correct the soil (the organic matter, the pH correction with lime or sulphur, and fertilizer) are applied at the same time.

The soil should be loosened to a depth of 6 to 8 inches. The corrective materials are spread over the loosened surface and then mixed into the loosened soil. A rotary tiller does this job most effectively.

▶ **Installing an Underground Sprinkler System**

There are several factors that determine where and how your underground sprinkler system is to be installed. The first part of this section will aid you in planning the layout and choosing the materials best suited for your particular sprinkler system. The remainder of the section contains procedures for working with different types of pipe and materials.

The main factor that determines layout of the system and amount of materials is the area of coverage required. Other factors involved are water pressure in your area, type of sprinkler head and piping.

It is a good idea for you to become familiar with the products on the market before making a choice as to pipe and sprinkler heads.

If you live in an extremely cold climate, check with a plumber about the depth to place system.

Your choice of piping will include galvanized iron, rigid (PVC) plastic or semi-rigid (poly) plastic. Be sure that the cement you use with plastic pipe is compatible with the plastic in the pipe (for example, ABS cement should not be used with PVC pipe).

The galvanized iron pipe resists damage caused by shovels or other yard work tools. However, it is more expensive and requires a greater amount of work to install. Each section needs to be cut, threaded and connected with a fitting.

The plastic pipe is much easier to work with because it can be cut with a hacksaw or sharp knife. Also, purchased fittings are secured to the pipe with a glue or cement. This eliminates the necessity for cutting pipe threads.

PVC must be installed in individual straight lengths, as with galvanized pipe. A fitting must also be installed at each change of direction.

The poly pipe can be bent, generally to a minimum of a 3-to-4-foot radius. Therefore, with proper planning, some fittings can be avoided with poly pipe.

Installing an Underground Sprinkler System

The most common types of sprinkler heads are the pulsating type, flush head and pop-up head. These are available in either metal or plastic. Most all heads are made with an adjustable spray pattern radius. Read the following descriptions before making a choice of sprinkler heads:

● Pulsating types [1] provide more water, therefore requiring fewer heads. They extend above ground farther than other types, causing a minor mowing or trimming problem. Pulsating type heads are available in full circle coverage or can be adjusted to a portion of the circle.

● Flush heads [2] can be installed even with the lawn or the tops of ground cover or flowers. They present less of a lawn mowing problem than the pulsating type, if installed correctly. Because of this they require careful installation to insure their proper elevation, especially if lawn or ground cover has not yet been installed.

● Pop-up heads [3] are similar to the flush heads with the added advantage that the elevation is not as critical.

Both the flush and pop-up head types are available in spray patterns that include full and partial circles, ovals, rectangles and squares.

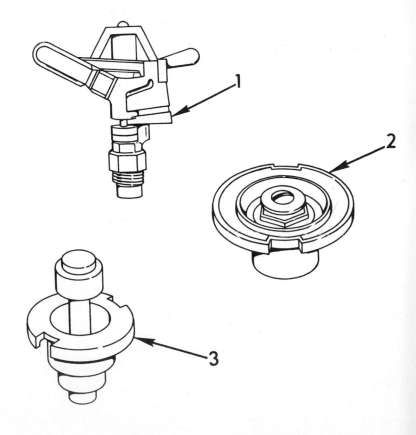

Installing an Underground Sprinkler System

Water supply pressure is measured with a pressure gage. If you do not have one and do not wish to buy one, your local water company may be able to help. Perform the following steps to determine water pressure using a gage:

1. Turn off main water shutoff valve [2].

2. Connect pressure gage [1] to outside water supply line.

3. Turn on valve [2]. Water pressure is measured in pounds per square inch (PSI). Read gage to determine water supply pressure.

This figure will determine number of sprinkler heads that can be supported with your water pressure for their proper operation.

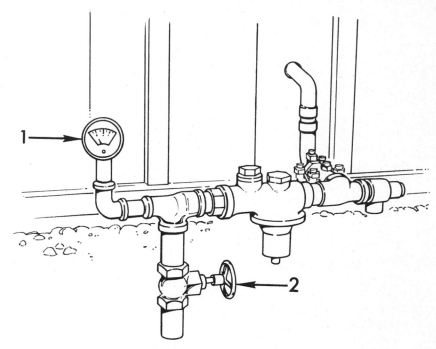

Installing an Underground Sprinkler System

Follow procedures below to determine the maximum number of sprinkler heads allowed on one line:

* Size of smallest diameter supply pipe between water meter and proposed sprinkler head must be known to select proper line in graph (1-in., 3/4-in. or 1/2-in.).

* Water pressure must be known. See section above.

* Manufacturer's rating of sprinkler head type that you have chosen must be known. Each make of sprinkler head is expressed in maximum flow of water in gallons per minute.

1. Using the graph, follow the 1/2-, 3/4-, or 1-inch line until it crosses the water pressure line.

2. Read straight across to the left to determine maximum flow per minute. Record this figure.

3. Divide figure obtained in Step 2 by sprinkler head rating.

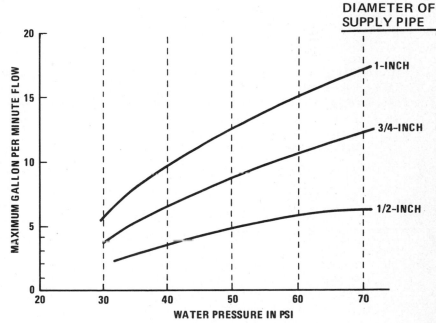

The figure obtained in Step 3 is the maximum number of sprinkler heads that should be installed on a length of pipe up to 100 feet long.

Installing an Underground Sprinkler System

Make a careful sketch on graph paper of the area that you want covered by sprinklers. Include accurate dimensions for locating all trees, flower beds and walks.

You should now have enough information to make a choice of sprinkler heads and pipe. In the example shown in this section, the following assumptions have been made:

- Area of coverage — as shown in illustration
- Type of sprinkler head — flush head with 3 gallon per minute flow by manufacturer's rating and a spray pattern radius of 12 feet adjustable to 2 feet.
- Water pressure — 60 PSI
- Water supply line — 1-inch
- Piping — semi-rigid plastic pipe

Follow the steps beginning on below as a guide when planning your sprinkler system.

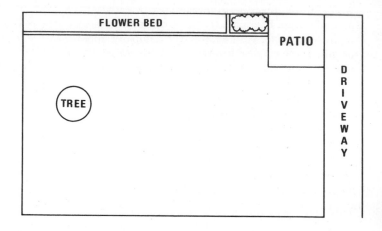

Installing an Underground Sprinkler System

1. Draw in sprinkler heads in each corner to insure that corners will be watered. In the example, there are five corners.

2. Corner heads, in most cases, will be one-quarter circles. Draw 12-foot arcs out from each sprinkler head.

3. Position edge sprinkler heads along all four sides until full coverage of edges is obtained. In example, four heads.

4. Position center heads until remaining coverage is obtained. In example, two heads.

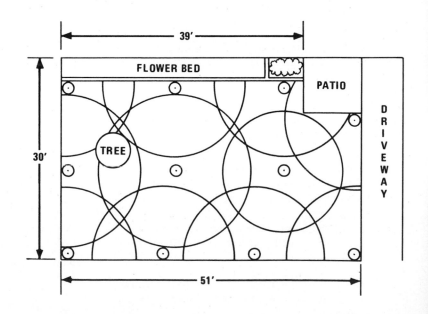

Installing an Underground Sprinkler System

The next step is to achieve complete coverage
using the minimum number of sprinkler heads.
This will save you labor and money — not only
on the heads but also the pipe and fitting.

5. Working with diagram on previous page,
    manipulate sprinkler heads around the lawn
    until minimum number are used for
    complete coverage.

You may want to cut a number of 1/4, 1/2
and full circles out of paper to move around on
the diagram. Be sure you find out all patterns
that are available in the type head you have
chosen.

In the example, sprinkler head placement has
been moved so that only seven heads have been
used, instead of eleven. Sprinkler [1] is called a
strip or parkway head. Sprinklers [2 and 3] may
be adjusted as desired to avoid as much over-
spray as possible.

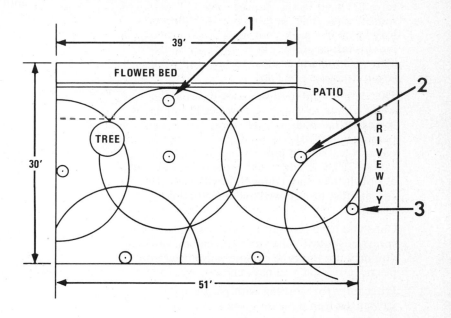

Installing an Underground Sprinkler System

The next step is to sketch in the pipe route,
using as few connections and bends as possible.
You should also consider the division of the
lawn when watering. It may be divided in almost
any way you want, as long as you do not exceed
the maximum number of heads per line.

Determine the desired position for sprinkler
valves — be sure they will be accessible when
water is on. Two possible divisions of the system
in the example are shown at right.

In the top illustration, the lawn area may be
watered next to the house, and then away from
the house. In lower illustration, the lawn is
divided approximately in half.

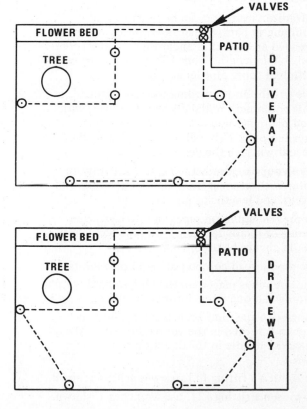

UTILITIES

Installing an Underground Sprinkler System

Each sprinkler line should include an anti-siphon valve [2] next to the shutoff valve [1]. A shutoff valve that contains an anti-siphon valve may be used. Check your local plumbing code for this information. These valves are installed above ground and as close to the supply line (from street) as possible.

There are several methods used to bring the water supply to the shutoff valves [1]. One of the easier methods is to tap directly from an outside faucet. However, do not attempt to connect a standard pipe thread fitting to the faucet. They are different types of thread, and although they may connect, it will leak. The faucet must be removed and a tee fitting installed.

Once you have brought the water supply to your sprinkler shutoff valves and anti-siphon valves, you may use the type of pipe, galvanized iron, plastic, etc., that you have chosen.

Procedures for working with plastic and galvanized iron pipe are given below. After purchasing all tools and materials needed, dig narrow trenches according to the final sprinkler layout. Trenches should be 8 inches deep if you are using 6-inch riser pipe [4] to allow for the elbow fitting [5] and sprinkler head [3].

Install your sprinkler system pipes and fittings in the trenches. Do not bury the pipe until the system has been tested for leaks and lawn coverage.

Follow your diagram as closely as possible for best results.

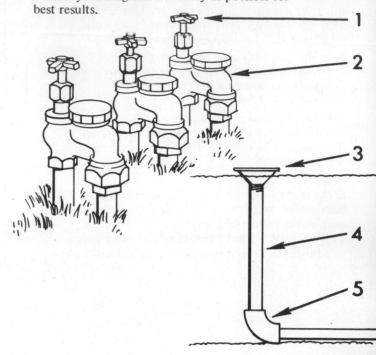

▶ Working with Steel Pipe

Galvanized iron pipe can be bought from plumbing or hardware dealers already cut and threaded as needed. Standard pipe nipples are available in lengths from 1 to 12 inches to make cutting of short pipe lengths unnecessary.

Pipe cutting and threading tools are available at most equipment rental dealers. However, with good planning, you can buy pre-cut and threaded pipe. This will be the easiest method to use and will give the best results.

Take your diagram with you to the hardware store. The salesman will help you determine all fittings and lengths of pipe required.

To prevent strain on pipes and fittings when joining or removing them, two pipe wrenches should always be used.

Use pipe thread compound on all pipe joints.

One wrench is placed on the pipe to hold it from turning and one wrench turns the fitting.

Damage to the pipe wrench can result if the wrench is turned in the wrong direction. Always move the handle in the direction of the open jaws.

To tighten a fitting [1], use wrenches as shown.

To loosen a fitting [2], use wrenches as shown.

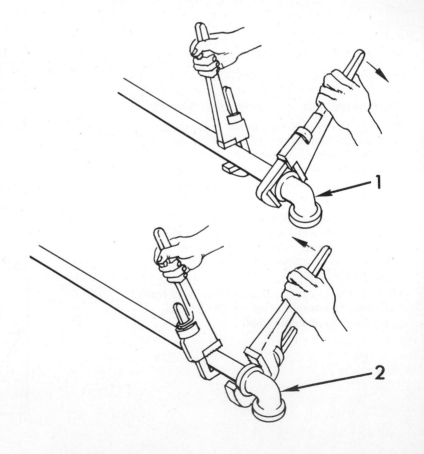

14

▶ **Working with Plastic Pipe**

1.   Measure and mark pipe [1] at desired length.

A straight cut is essential to prevent possible leaks when pipe is connected into the system.

2.   Place pipe [1] into miter box. Using hacksaw or sharp knife, cut pipe straight through at mark.

3.   Using half-round file, remove any burrs and rough edges from inside cut end of pipe [1].

4.   Using sandpaper, remove any burrs and rough edges from outside cut end of pipe [1].

Follow manufacturer's instructions for applying solvent cement. Solvent cements come in one-step and two-step types. Some types cannot be applied below specific temperatures.

5.   Before applying cement to plain fittings, insert pipe [3] into fitting [2]. Check that pipe butts squarely against inner shoulder of fitting. If not, sandpaper the outside of pipe to facilitate fit. Do not remove more plastic than necessary.

6.   Remove pipe [3] from fitting [2].

7.   If using a two-step cement, apply cleaning solvent to mating surfaces of pipe [3] and fitting [2].

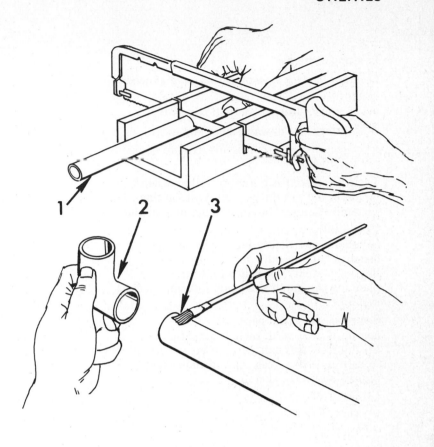

Working with Plastic Pipe

Read the instructions on the cement container before continuing. Many cements set up quickly; time between application and completion of the joint is very short.

8.   Using brush, apply cement to mating surfaces of pipe [2] and fitting [1].

Pipe or fitting is turned 1/4 turn after they are joined. Be sure fitting is left pointing in the desired direction.

9.   Insert pipe [2] into fitting [1] until end of pipe butts squarely against inner shoulder of fitting. Turn pipe or fitting 1/4 turn. Hold fitting in place for about a minute to keep joint together until glue takes hold.

Follow instructions on cement container for allowing joint to set.

10. Apply PVC cement to any threaded fittings to increase probability of having the joint seal properly. Also, cement will act as a lubricant and facilitate screwing the fitting to the pipe or adjacent fitting.

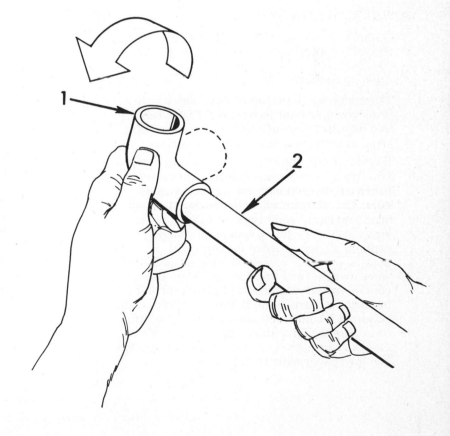

▶ **Lighting Systems**

Outdoor lighting systems satisfy several needs and uses.

- Utility — eating and patio areas
- Safety — walkways, steps and gates
- Security — entrances and exits to house and yard

There are three basic steps to follow when selecting and installing an outdoor lighting system: Planning, buying the lighting kit and installation.

If you are sufficiently knowledgeable to construct and install your own home-made lighting system, you may wish to use the planning paragraph as a guide to laying out the system.

Planning. On graph paper, accurately draw the layout of your yard. Include all patio areas, shrubs, trees and exits, even if you do not intend to light up these areas. Also include exact dimensions in the sketch.

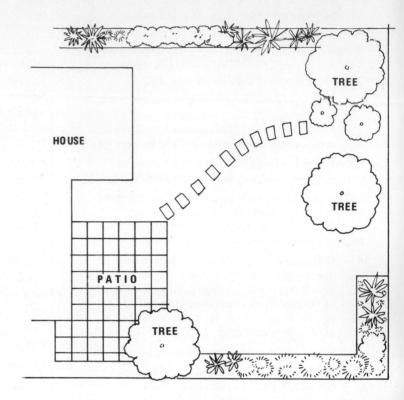

Lighting Systems

Determine which individual items and which areas you may want to highlight. Lights may also be installed at different heights on poles, trees, or even suspended from wire or lines.

Buying the lighting kit. Take your sketch with you to your local home improvement center or hardware store. Don't hesitate to consult a salesman. They know, or can tell you someone who does know, what types of lighting systems are available. A lighting system kit generally contains all items needed for complete installation. They contain lighting fixtures, wires, switches and transformers. They also contain special recommended placement and installation instructions. Before purchasing a kit, be sure it is compatible with your local electrical code. Buy the kit with enough wire and one or two extra fixtures (you may need more than one kit) for your specific layout.

Installation. After you have purchased the kit, lay the entire system out before applying power. Leave enough slack in the wires to permit movement of fixtures. After the system is in the desired position, apply power according to the manufacturer's instructions. You should check out the lighting effects both at dusk and during darkness. After you have decided on the exact placement of all fixtures, secure them to the required poles, trees or ground stakes.

Using the proper tools for a job will make the work easier.

You must acquire a certain tool inventory to properly plant or maintain your landscape.

Although many tools are versatile, very often it is difficult to substitute one tool for another, or to use a tool for other than its intended use.

When selecting gardening tools, shop for the best quality your budget will allow.

Although cheap tools will get the job done, they will not stay sharp, will corrode easily, will be difficult to maneuver or manipulate and will be a bother to maintain.

You don't need to buy all of your tools at once, but you will need some basics to start with. Add others as you need them.

Some tools that are used rarely may be rented from your nursery supply center.

The chart lists the tools and their uses. The most common tools are listed first. The bottom portion lists tools for special jobs.

LAWN AND GARDEN TOOLS

	Lawns	Ground Covers	Trees and Shrubs	Gardens
Hose [1]	●	●	●	●
Nozzle [2]	●	●	●	●
Mower [3]	●	●		
Round End Shovel [4]			●	●
Bow Rake [5]	●	●		●
Hoe [6]		●		●
Pruning Shears [7]			●	●
Sprinkler [8]	●	●		●
Spading Fork [9]		●		●
Sprayer [10]	●	●	●	●
Trowel [11]		●		●
Square End Shovel [12]			●	●
Leaf Rake [13]	●	●		
Grass Shears [14]	●	●		●
Edger [15]	●	●		
Pruning Saw [16]			●	
Lopping Shears [17]			●	
Hedge Shears [18]			●	●
Spreader [19]	●	●		
Root Feeder [20]			●	

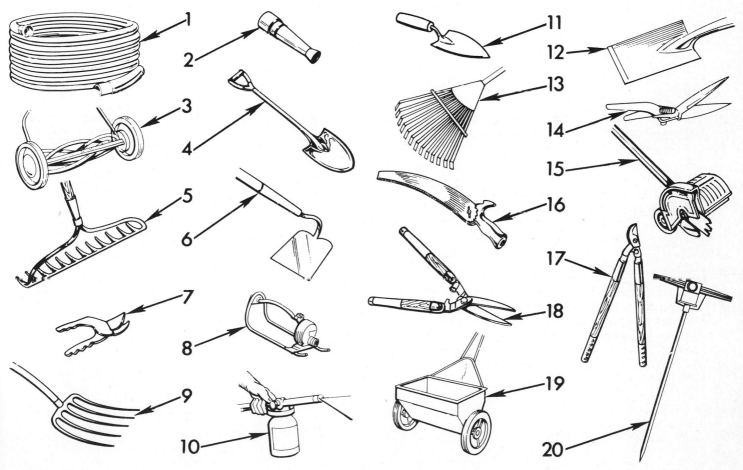

When selecting a garden hose, there are four things to keep in mind:

- Construction – reinforced construction can withstand pressure surges up to 20 times normal water pressure, and withstand temperatures well below freezing. Nonreinforced construction will break.

- Diameter – 5/8-inch can deliver half again as much flow rate as 1/2-inch hose. 3/4-inch hose can deliver twice the flow rate of 1/2-inch hose, with water pressures equal.

- Material – rubber has flexibility and strength. Plastic is vinyl and rubber blended to combine flexibility with strength.

- Length – most are available in 25-, 50-, or 75-foot lengths. Choose one that will suit your needs.

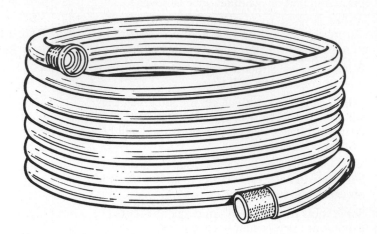

When selecting a spreader, there are three things to consider:

- A trough-type spreader [1] gives a more even distribution than a broadcast-type spreader [2], but work goes faster with a broadcast type. This may be of interest if your yard is large.

- Select a spreader with on/off and distribution rate controls. Controls should be within easy reach during operation.

- Select a spreader that has corrosion-resistant parts. Easy cleaning, lubricating and maintenance are also important to the long service life of your spreader.

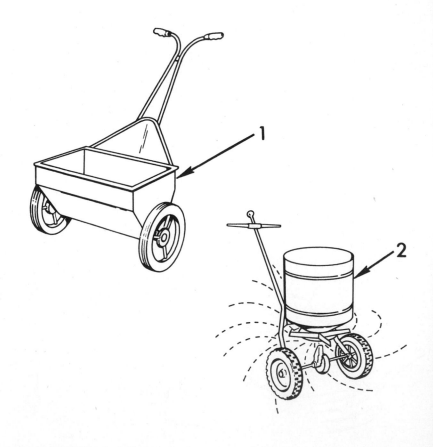

When selecting a mower, consider:

● A heavy mower will be difficult and tiring to use, especially on sloping or uneven surfaces. A heavy mower will also contribute to compacting the soil.

● Cutting blades must be sharp and must be strong enough to withstand an occasional stick, stone or bone.

● Large wheels distribute the weight of the mower over a larger area, and will also make maneuvering over rough surface easier.

● Reel-type mowers with low gear ratio, or less than 5 blades, may leave a wavey appearance.

● Reel-type mowers can be adjusted to cut very low but not high. Rotary mowers can be adjusted to cut very high but not low. Height of cut will depend on the kind of grass.

● Cleaning, lubricating and routine maintenance activities are important to the service life of a mower.

There are many different kinds of sprinklers from which to choose:

● Oscillating sprinklers [1] can be adjusted to full or partial water throw settings.

● Pulsating sprinklers [2] can be adjusted from fixed position to a full circle.

● Rotary sprinklers [3] usually are adjustable only by regulating the flow rate. Some are equipped with deflectors that permit square patterns or circular patterns.

● Traveling sprinklers [4] are usually rotary sprinklers that use flowing water to drive a set of wheels. The sprinkler follows the lay of the hose. Another type of traveling sprinkler winds up a cord that is staked along the route the sprinkler is to follow.

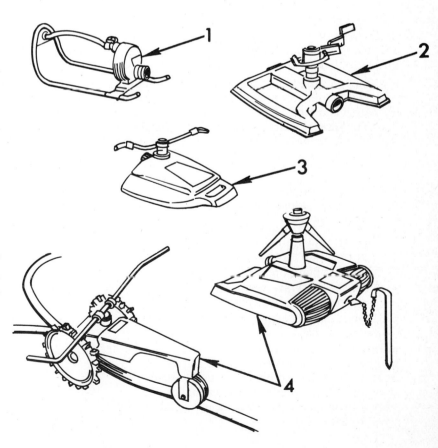

TOOLS AND SUPPLIES

Shovels are used to move dirt or other bulky material. Short-handled shovels are used where the work is light, or room is restricted, so that a long-handled shovel cannot be used.

The top of the shovel is flat so that the foot may be used to drive the edge into the material to be moved. A shovel [1, 3] is usually hollowed out as contrasted to a spade [2] which has a flat blade. The edge of a shovel can be kept sharp by filing. If the edge becomes deformed, place shovel on a flat, hard surface and beat it back into shape, then sharpen the edge.

Shovels and spades come in various widths. The narrow ones [1] are used for narrow or limited width digging. Wider shovels [3] are used for larger projects.

Rounded, pointed shovels make digging into hard surfaces easier. Flat, square-ended shovels make removing material from a flat surface easier.

Shovels should be cleaned after use. Cleanup is easy using a wire brush or steel wool and plenty of water. After cleaning, apply a coat of oil, grease or wax to metal parts to prevent corrosion. A coat of paint will prevent corrosion if the item is to be stored for a long period of time.

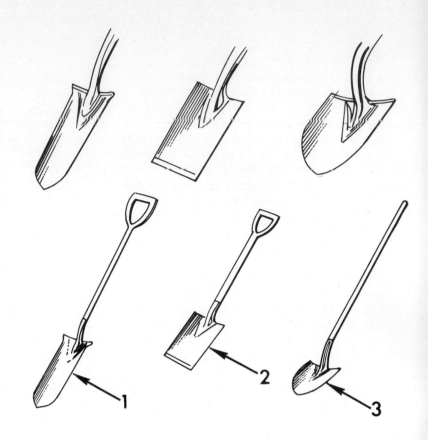

Sprayers are used to distribute liquid pesticides and fertilizers. Your nursery supply center has different kinds of sprayers to choose from.

- Siphon type [1]. To use this type, fill bowl with liquid according to directions on the label and attach the nozzle to your hose. The flow of water through the nozzle will siphon the liquid from the bowl, dilute it to proper concentration and apply it to whatever you are spraying.

- Compressed air sprayers [2] are equipped with an air pump that is used to pressurize the container. Flow is controlled by a shut-off valve and an adjustable nozzle. The nozzle is usually adjustable from a stream to a fine spray. A shoulder strap is provided to make the sprayer easy to carry. Compressed air sprayers are considerably more expensive than the siphon-type sprayer.

Sprayers should be made of non-corrosive materials since pesticides and fertilizers are normally highly corrosive. Routine cleaning will also help to control corrosion and add to the service life of the equipment. Follow instructions in manufacturer's service manual or owner's manual for servicing, cleaning and maintaining sprayers.

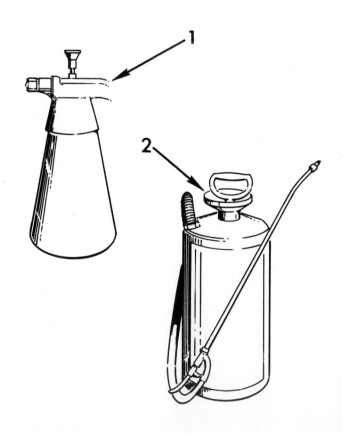

When selecting pesticides, fertilizers, seed, etc., keep in mind that the unused portion must be stored somewhere.

Purchase your supplies only in large enough volumes to accomplish your immediate needs.

Leftover seeds may be kept in a closed container (i.e. a coffee can or some similar container) for a limited period of time. Fresh seed has a high probability of germination, but as seeds grow older, the probability of germination decreases. Seed more than 18 months old should not be used because of unsatisfactory results.

Pesticides, such as herbicides, insecticides and fungicides, are poisons, and should be stored in their original containers. The container has identification of contents and antidote information printed on it.

Select poisons that are packaged in non-breakable containers and store them in a locked cabinet and out of the reach of children and pets.

Whichever product you purchase, be sure you read all warnings and information on the label before using and storing.

The following warnings should always be observed:

WARNING

Do not breathe fumes and vapors from an aerosol spray can.

If mixing, prepare only the amount needed for immediate use.

Do not use flammables or aerosols near an open flame.

Wash all containers thoroughly before disposing of them. Use detergent and water.

Always read cautions and warnings on all labels.

LAWNS

Careful consideration should be given to selecting the type of grass to be planted. A description of the types of grasses most frequently used for lawns begins on Page 25. These descriptions will help you to make your selection.

You must consider the existence of factors in your area which will affect how successfully a selected grass can be grown on your lawn. The factors which will influence how well your selection will grow are:

- Soil Conditions — some grasses will tolerate poor soil better than others.

- Climate — amount of rainfall, average summer and winter temperatures, amount of sunshine and wind conditions.

- Site — on steep slopes, a grass may be difficult or dangerous to mow and maintain. In such cases, a ground cover may be a better choice.

In addition to factors which will affect how well your grass selection will grow on your lot, there are other factors that will affect your selection.

- Durability — resistance to weeds, disease and heavy wear.

- Maintenance — requirements for frequent fertilizing, mowing, weeding, dethatching, etc.

- Appearance — however, fine-textured lawns require more care.

- Cost — some grasses cannot be planted from seed and cost more to install. Some require dethatching and fertilizing which results in additional expense as well as effort.

- Method of Planting — you may have a preference relating to this factor. See Methods of Planting, Page 29.

- Time of Year for Planting — you may be unwilling to delay planting.

Hybrids of each of the types of grasses discussed later in this section are continually being developed. These hybrids are improved strains intended to overcome weaknesses the grasses may have.

Plan to spend some time with a reputable nurseryman or grower before making a final decision. They should know which grasses do best in your area, the newest developments in each type of grass and what time of year to plant your selection.

A mixture of no more than 3 or 4 kinds of grasses is generally recommended. The advantage of a mix is that each type of grass will generally take over the areas where it performs better than the others, such as shady spots.

Caution should be taken in selecting mixtures. Some mixes contain a large amount of quick-growing cover grasses, such as rye. In the past, it was thought that these grasses held the soil while the slower-growing, fine grasses got established. It is now thought that these grasses rob the soil of the nutrients needed to promote healthy growth of the desired grasses. Also, the seeds of the quick-growing grasses tend to be large and bulky and reduce the number of desired grass seeds per pound. These mixes may seem less expensive, but they are not.

Grasses generally fall into two categories. The selection of an applicable category is influenced by the general climate map. Both the cool-season and warm-season categories contain several types of grasses. A brief description of these types of grasses follows.

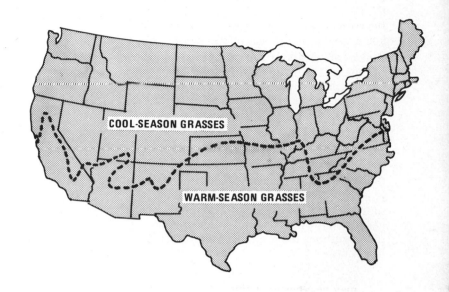

► **Cool-Season Grasses**

- BENT GRASSES have a very fine appearance but require high maintenance, i.e., close mowing, fertilizing, watering and disease control. They are cut to a height of 1/2 to 3/4 inch.

- FINE FESCUES have a fine-textured appearance. They blend well with other grasses and are more tolerant of poor soil conditions. They are cut to a height of 1-1/2 to 2 inches.

- BLUE GRASSES are the most popular and best all-around lawn in the cool-season area. They are heat and drought resistant, and require medium maintenance. They do not grow in shade. They are cut to a height of 1-1/2 inches.

Cool-Season Grasses

- RYE GRASSES grow in bunches and cannot produce a tight, even lawn. They can be used as a temporary ground cover. Small amounts can be used in a mix on slopes to prevent soil erosion while desired grasses get established. They are cut to a height of 1-1/2 to 2 inches.

- COARSE FESCUES do not have a fine appearance and are generally used for football fields and other high-use areas. They are tough, durable and drought resistant. They are cut to a height of 1-1/2 to 2 inches.

► **Warm-Season Grasses (Subtropical)**

- ZOYSIA GRASSES produce a dense turf with no weeds, insects or diseases. A single header board will contain them. They will grow in some shade. They are slow–growing and take 1 to 3 years for turf to become solid. They go dormant and turn brown with the first frost. They are planted as plugs or stolens. They are cut low to a height of 1/2 inch.

- ST. AUGUSTINE GRASSES provide a solid turf in 1 year that is weed-free. They are susceptible to some diseases and have a very coarse appearance. They will withstand shade and salt spray. They require yearly dethatching. They are cut low to a height of 1/2 inch.

- BERMUDA GRASSES provide a fine-textured lawn that takes heavy wear. They resist weeds and some diseases. They brown with winter frost and require medium maintenance. They are the most popular lawn in warm-winter areas. They are cut low to a height of 1/2 inch.

- DICHONDRA is not a grass. It is a low-growing ground cover used extensively in Arizona and California. It is very attractive, but it will not take heavy wear. It requires regular feeding and watering. It does not need frequent mowing. It is cut only if it is higher than 2 inches.

▶ Preparing the Site

Read the section on Planting a Lawn, Pages 26–38, before beginning any work. There are several choices of methods for planting lawns and the equipment required will vary depending on the method you choose. You will want to have these equipment items on hand before you begin work.

Before starting to work, select the type of grass you want and make sure it is the correct time of year for planting that type of grass.

In order to grow a healthy and attractive lawn, you must first determine the condition of the soil, and the correct amounts of additives you need to mix with the soil. Without the proper soil conditions the results of your efforts could be a scrawny lawn. Be sure to read Soil Conditions beginning on Page 8. Purchase the required soil additives before you start to work.

To prepare the lawn bed, the soil must be loosened to a depth of 6 to 10 inches.

If the soil is dry and hard, water the area at least a day in advance. The soil should be moist and easily workable. You can check with a spade or shovel to determine the condition of the soil. If the soil is too dry, the spade will not easily reach the 6- to 10-inch depth. Water again until the soil is moist to the proper depth.

If the soil is too wet, it will stick to the shovel and cling together in large clods. These clods will not break up easily. If the soil is too wet, wait another day. Check again to see if the soil has reached the moist and workable condition.

If desired, this check could be done a week or two before you plan to prepare the bed. This will help you determine how long it takes for the soil to reach the desired workability after watering. You can then plan to do the work when you are ready.

Preparing the Site

Loosening the soil can be accomplished with a standard, square-end spade or with a gasoline-powered rotary tiller. Unless the area is very small, you should use a rotary tiller. A rotary tiller can be rented at most equipment rental agencies or nurseries. The rotary tiller will save time and work and do a good job of mixing soil additives into the soil.

If you decide to rent a rotary tiller, be sure to have the salesman show you how to operate it and how to set the cutting depth of the blades.

If you plan to till with a spade, go to bottom of Page 27.

If using a rotary tiller, continue.

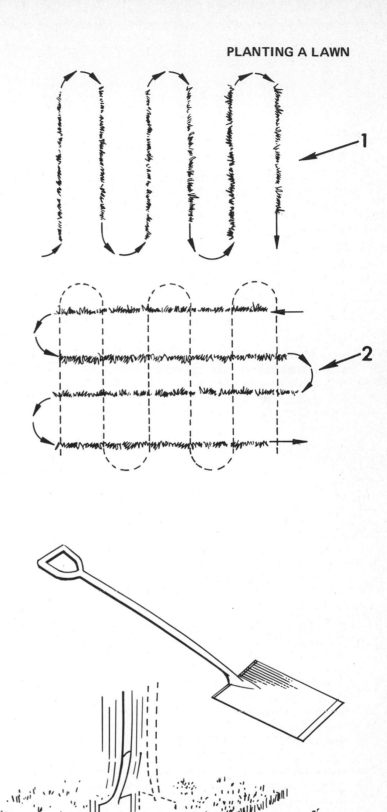

Preparing the Site

If there is light growth of grass or weeds or no growth in the lawn area, go to Step 3.

If there is heavy grass and weed growth in the lawn area, continue.

1.   Set the cutting depth on the rotary tiller to 1 or 2 inches.

2.   Using the rotary tiller, work back and forth in one direction [1] and then work back and forth in a cross direction [2].

This will chop up turf fine enough to be mixed into the soil in the loosening operation.

3.   Set the cutting depth on the rotary tiller to 6 inches.

4.   Using the rotary tiller, work back and forth in one direction [1] and then work back and forth in a cross direction [2].

5.   Go to Page 28, Step 4.

Preparing the Site

Using hoe, cut any heavy growth of weeds and grasses in the lawn area. Remove both the roots and growth from the lawn area. Roots and growth cannot be broken up sufficiently to allow mixing into the soil with the hand method.

A standard spade with a square end is the most effective tool to use in tilling the soil by hand. The spade should be held in a vertical position and pushed straight into the soil. Rock the spade and lift up the soil.

1.   Using the standard spade, dig a trench the width of the spade and 10 inches deep across one end of the lawn bed. Place soil out of the way to be used later.

Preparing the Site

2. Dig another trench the width of the spade and 10 inches deep next to the first trench. Turn the soil on its side into the first trench. Do not turn the soil upside down.

Repeat Step 2 until the other end of the lawn bed is reached.

3. Using the soil removed in Step 1, fill in the last trench.

4. Using an iron rake, break up and smooth soil. Remove stones, root clods, sticks and other debris. Some of this debris will have to be picked out by hand.

5. Using spade or rake, spread the soil additives over tilled area, if required.

Preparing the Site

6. Spread a complete fertilizer over the tilled area.

7. Using spade and rake or rotary tiller, mix additives and fertilizer into the soil.

If using rotary tiller to mix the additives and fertilizers into the soil, use the same criss-cross method which was used to loosen the soil.

Make sure the soil and additives are thoroughly mixed and you cannot see different layers of materials in the soil. This prevents problems in later years. A well-mixed soil allows nutrients, water and oxygen to reach the grass roots.

8. Using a rake held at a low angle, smooth the lawn area. The low angle prevents forming hollows and low spots.

Preparing the Site

If the soil is very loose so that walking on it creates footprints 2 to 3 inches deep, it will not hold moisture properly. Footprints should be only 1/2 inch deep. Loose soil can be firmed by watering the area and letting it settle overnight or by rolling it with an empty roller.

Rollers are available for rent at most garden supply stores, equipment rental agencies or nurseries. If using a roller, it is easier to push the roller ahead of you than to pull it.

If watering the area, water with a fine spray. Stop watering when puddles begin to form or water runs off the area.

Using a wooden ladder with a rope tied to one side or two planks nailed together with a rope attached, draw the lawn bed to level out low spots and remove bumps. This will prevent puddling and assure proper drainage.

If the lawn area is next to the house, be sure soil is higher near the house and slopes gently away.

Lawn bed is now ready to plant.

▶ Methods of Planting

Your choice of a method of planting your lawn may depend on the type of grass you are planting. Some grasses cannot be planted from seed. Plugs or sprigs of these grasses must be planted.

Other considerations for choosing the method of planting are cost, type of site (e.g., a steep bank may be subject to erosion from heavy rainfall and warrant the use of sod or plugs in lieu of seed) or your desire for solid coverage for appearance.

Seeding is the most inexpensive way to plant a lawn. For those grasses that are slow to establish, your nurseryman can suggest a combination of seeds to provide fast coverage while the basic grass is getting established. Remember that the quick-growing cover grasses may rob the soil of nutrients needed to promote healthy growth of the desired grasses. Thus, in the long run, it may pay to accept a delay in having a green lawn in the interests of a healthy lawn.

Sprigs are runners of grass plants that generally cannot be planted by seed. Sprigs are planted and they spread out to cover the lawn.

Planting sprigs, like seeding, can be inexpensive. The rate of coverage will depend on how closely the sprigs are planted.

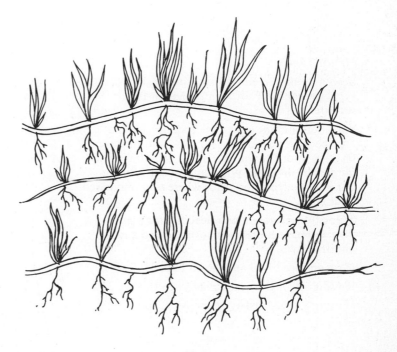

SPRIGS

PLANTING A LAWN

Methods of Planting

Plugs [1] are small sections of established grass grown in flat boxes or cut from a bed of grass. The plugs are planted and the grass in the plugs spreads to cover the lawn. This method is slightly more expensive that planting sprigs. However, plugs are easier to handle than sprigs.

Sod [2] is strips of established grass cut from a grass bed. The strips are usually 12 inches wide and up to 6 feet long. Planting sod provides an "instant" lawn, but is expensive. Sod has definite advantages on steep slopes where seeds could be washed away by watering or rainfall. A combination of sodding and seeding or another method of planting could be considered if part of your lawn area has banks or slopes.

If selecting any method of planting other than seeding, planning your work is very important. The sprigs, plugs or sod must be kept moist until planting or they will die. Purchase or have the materials delivered on the morning you plan to plant.

If planting seed, go to next section (below).

If planting sprigs, go to Page 34.

If planting plugs, go to Page 35.

If planting sod, go to Page 36.

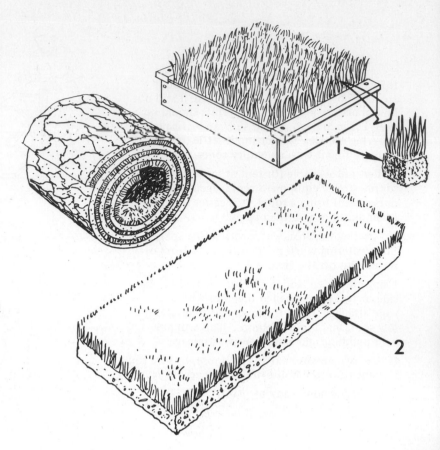

▶ Planting Seed

Seed may be spread by hand sowing, by a trough-type spreader [1], or by a broadcast-type spreader [2].

Spreaders are not expensive to purchase and may be used year after year to spread fertilizer or to re-seed if required. If you do not wish to purchase a spreader you can probably rent or borrow one from the place where you purchased your seed.

If possible, choose a windless day for planting. You will have more even coverage and a more uniform lawn.

If sowing seed by hand, go to Page 31.

If using a trough-type spreader, go to Page 31.

If using a broadcast-type spreader, go to Page 32.

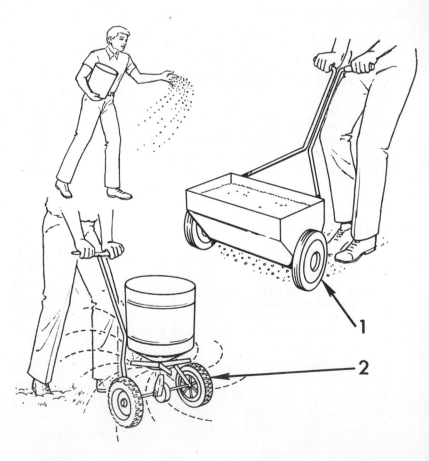

▶ Planting Seed by Hand

1. Divide the amount of seed required to cover the size of the lawn area into 4 equal parts.

2. Mix each part of seed with one or two cups of dry sand or topsoil. The sand or topsoil will serve as a carrier for the seed.

3. Using stakes and strings, divide the lawn into 4 sections [1].

4. Scatter the seed by throwing it from your hand in a wide arc [3] in front of you. Follow the pattern shown [2] sowing one of the four parts of seed on each path. This will help provide even coverage over the area.

5. Using the back of a leaf rake, lightly drag the rake over the seeded area to barely cover the seed.

6. Rope off area with stakes and strings to prevent foot traffic, if necessary.

7. Water seed. Page 33.

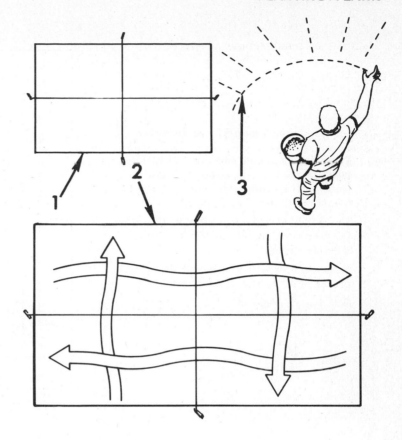

▶ Planting Seed with a Trough-Type Spreader

A trough-type spreader distributes the seed through adjustable holes in the bottom of the trough. Directions for setting the openings should be included with the manufacturer's instructions. Look for the proper setting to use on the seed package.

1. Adjust the openings in the trough according to manufacturer's instructions for the type of seed you are using. If in doubt about the correct setting, check with the store where you purchased the spreader.

2. Place seed in spreader and spread out evenly across the trough.

3. Spread a row or two of seed across each end of lawn area, making sure to turn the spreader off while making a turn. Overlap each row 1 to 2 inches to prevent spaces without seeds.

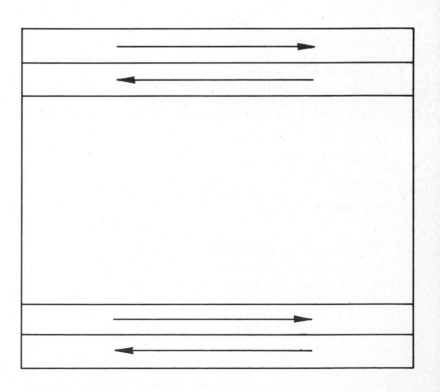

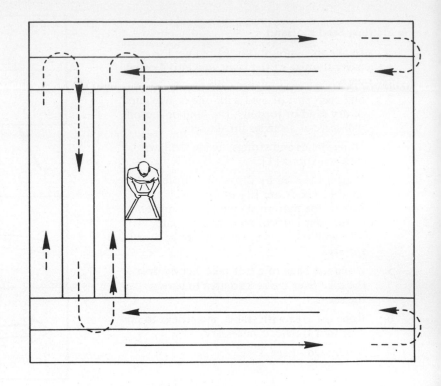

Planting Seed with Trough-Type Spreader

4. Spread rows of seed in a cross direction until the lawn area is covered. Remember to turn off spreader while turning and to overlap each row 1 to 2 inches.

5. Using the back of a leaf rake, lightly drag the rake over the seeded area to barely cover the seed.

6. Rope off area with stakes and strings to prevent foot traffic, if necessary.

7. Water seed. Page 33.

▶ **Planting Seed with Broadcast-Type Spreader**

A broadcast-type spreader drops the seed through a single adjustable hole onto a spinning disk. This spinning disk forces the seed out in an arc 8 to 12 feet wide. The speed at which you walk determines how far the seed is thrown. The wheel controls the disk so the faster you walk, the faster the disk spins, and the farther the seed is thrown.

The important thing to remember is to walk at a steady speed to insure that the seed is spread evenly.

The manufacturer's instructions should tell you how to adjust the rate of seed and what setting to use for the type of seed you are planting.

The seed package may also give the setting for each type spreader.

1. Adjust the hole to the proper spreading rate.

2. Load spreader.

Planting Seed with Broadcast-Type Spreader

In the next step, be sure to overlap each path generously to assure good coverage.

3. Beginning in one corner of the lawn area, spread seed back and forth across the area [1]

4. Beginning in the opposite corner of the lawn area, spread seed back and forth across the area [2] in a direction at a right angle to the one used in Step 3.

5. Using the back of a leaf rake [3], lightly drag the rake over the seeded area to barely cover the seed.

6. Rope off area with stakes and strings to prevent foot traffic, if necessary.

7. Water seed. See next section (below).

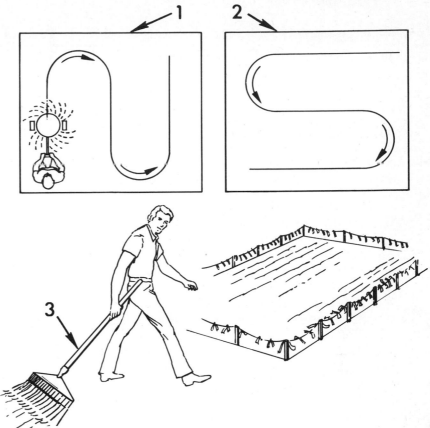

▶ **Watering Seed**

Watering a newly planted seed bed requires different handling than other planting methods.

The seeded area MUST be kept dark with moisture until the seeds have germinated and all the grass is up. This may require watering several times a day in hot weather.

CAUTION

Do not apply so much water that the seeds wash away.

Do not walk on the seeded area until the grass is about 2 inches high.

If the lawn area is small and you can reach all parts of it without turning the hose on so hard that it washes away seeds, laying out a watering system will not be necessary. However, it will save you some time if you don't have to hand water as often as required to keep the area moist.

There are several types of portable sprinklers you might want to use. Once you place the portable sprinkling system so that all areas of the seed bed are reached, leave them there until the grass is about 2 inches high. Any marks made by hoses will disappear shortly — after you remove the hoses.

Read procedures on Page 37 for watering the new lawn.

▶ **Planting Sprigs**

If you elect to plant with sprigs, the sprigs must not be allowed to dry out. If planting is interrupted for any reason, place the sprigs in a plastic bag, add a small amount of water and place the bag out of the sun. Continue planting the sprigs as soon as possible.

The soil should be moist, but not so wet that it sticks together.

Planting sprigs may be easier if stakes and strings are used as guides [1]. These lines should be about 12 inches apart. If desired, for faster coverage the lines can be closer together but this will require more sprigs.

To plant a lawn with sprigs, proceed as follows:

1. Using a hoe or similar garden tool, make shallow V-shaped trenches [2] across the lawn area following the guide lines [1]. The trenches should be about 3 inches deep.

2. Place sprig [3] in trench at a slight angle so that some leaves on one of the sprigs are above the soil surface and the leaves on the other end will be buried.

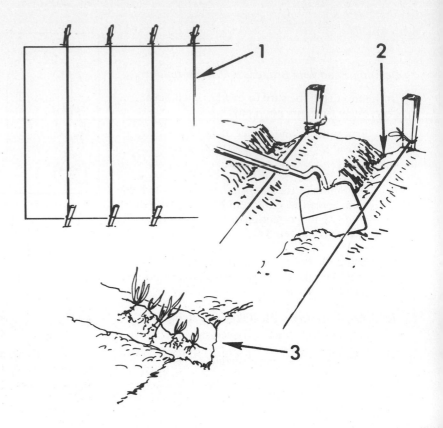

Planting Sprigs

3. Hold the sprig in place with one hand while filling in trench with the other hand. Gently press soil into firm contact with roots of sprig.

4. Repeat Steps 2 and 3 until lawn area is covered.

5. Using a rake, gently smooth out area between sprigs.

6. Rope off the area with stakes and strings to prevent foot traffic, if necessary.

Newly planted sprigs must be kept moist until the roots are established and the plants begin to grow. Watering should be done gently to prevent washing the dirt away from the sprigs.

Go to Page 37 for watering procedure.

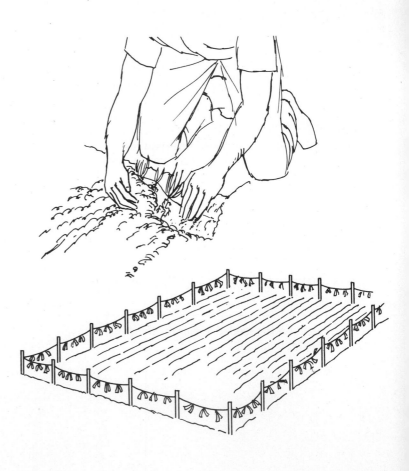

▶ **Planting Plugs**

If you elect to plant with plugs, the soil should be moist but not so moist that it sticks together.

Plugs are generally planted 12 inches apart, but can be spaced 6 or 8 inches apart for faster coverage. This requires more grass plants to cover the lawn area.

A grid [1] can be marked on the prepared soil bed with a board with nails driven partly through it. The nails are spaced at the interval you choose. The board is dragged across the area and the extended nails will mark the soil.

1. Using plugging tool [2] or garden trowel [3], make holes in soil large enough and deep enough to hold the plugs with grass portion above the surface of the surrounding soil. Make the holes at the intersections of the grid lines [1].

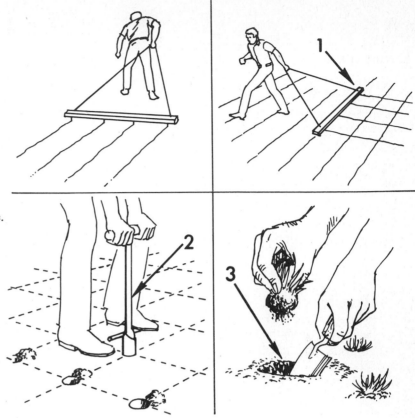

Planting Plugs

2. Place a small amount of water in each hole and let it drain into the soil.

If desired, you can now add a spoonful of organic fertilizer to each hole. Mix it with the dirt in the bottom of the holes. This will help the plants grow faster.

3. Using knife or plugging tool, cut grass into 2 to 4 inch squares.

4. Place one plug in each hole.

5. Firmly press the plug into the hole to assure soil is in contact with the roots of the plug.

6. Using rake, gently smooth the soil between the plugs.

7. Rope off area with stakes and strings to prevent foot traffic, if necessary.

Go to Page 37 for watering procedure.

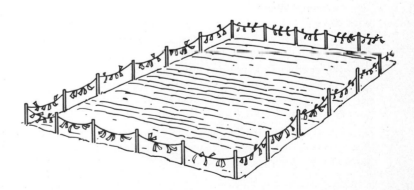

▶ Planting Sod

Planting with sod will result in a solid green lawn the day it is planted.

If lawn area is curved, laying sod may be easier if stakes and strings are used to make straight lines for use as guides.

If the lawn area is next to the pavement, be sure the soil is low enough along the pavement so that roots are below pavement level and the grass leaves are above the pavement level.

1. Lay sod across one end of lawn. Place pieces of sod end to end with as little space between pieces as possible.

2. Check that sod is smooth and even. If not, roll back and add or remove soil as required.

3. Place a broad board on the first strip of sod and work from the board to prevent compacting the unsodded soil.

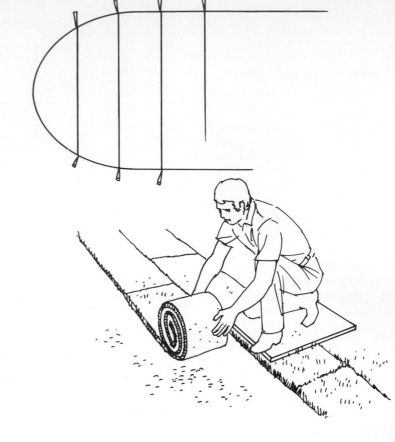

Planting Sod

4. Lay the next row of sod. Place pieces of sod end to end with as little space between pieces as possible.

The joints between pieces of sod should be staggered [1].

5. Moving the board with you as you work, repeat Steps 1 and 2 until the area is covered.

6. Fill gaps between pieces of sod with soil.

The roots of the sod must be in firm contact with the soil. This can be accomplished with a half-full roller [2], a tamping tool [3], or a board [4] that is tapped with a mallet.

7. Water the newly planted lawn area thoroughly. Water once or twice a week for 4 to 8 weeks. If the sod appears wilted and footprints do not spring, water the sod.

After 4 to 8 weeks it is necessary to encourage deep rooting of the grass. Read Page 38 for the normal watering procedure.

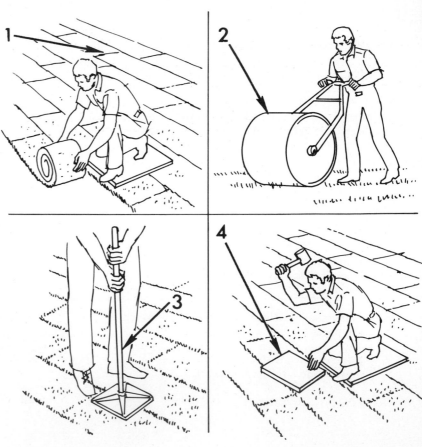

▶ Watering the New Lawn

A newly planted lawn requires careful watering. Improper watering will wash away seeds and small grass plants.

Water should fall gently on the area so that it does not

- Wash across the area carrying soil, seeds or plants with it.
- Splash the soil from the seeds or plant roots.
- Form puddles.

Keep the area moist, but not wet. If the area becomes too wet, you may have problems with disease or insects at a later time. Wait for the lawn area to develop light spots and then water until the entire area becomes evenly dark with moisture.

This may require watering several times a day in hot weather or not watering on some overcast cool days.

Since you will be watering frequently while establishing the lawn, weeds may become a problem.

Do not weed the seeded lawn areas until all the grass has come up. When pulling weeds on a new lawn, use a flat board for kneeling to distribute your weight.

In areas planted with sprigs or plugs, gently hoe between plantings or weed by hand. Do not pull the weeds growing very close to the new plants. You would disturb their roots.

Do not apply weed killers during the first growing season. Weed killers could injure your plants.

Watering may be done by hand, with portable sprinklers or using a permanently installed sprinkler system.

Several examples of portable sprinklers are shown below.

Watering the New Lawn

Example 1 shows a perforated hose which distributes a fine mist through the holes. The advantage of this method is that it can be shaped to fit oddly shaped areas.

Example 2 shows an oscillating sprinkler. The water is distributed through holes in the cross bar at the top of the sprinkler. This cross bar moves slowly to place water in a rectangular shape and can be adjusted for different patterns.

Example 3 shows a turret sprinkler. This sprinkler has multiple heads with small holes in each head. It sends out water in a steady spray to give a lot of water in a short time. The heads can be adjusted for different patterns.

Example 4 shows one way of setting up several sprinklers to cover a large area. Hoses are connected using inexpensive Y-joints available at hardware stores.

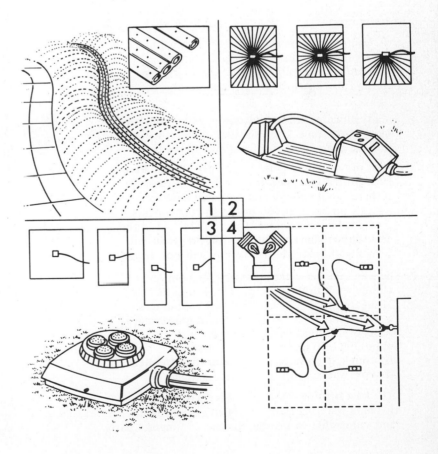

▶ Cutting the New Lawn

A new lawn may require mowing before the root system is fully developed. Wait until the grass is at least half again as high as the recommended minimum cutting height for the type of grass you selected. Then cut no shorter than recommended and preferably slightly higher.

Adjust the height of the mower on a sidewalk or other flat surface.

Let the lawn area dry out enough so that the mower wheels will not leave ruts or tear the grass.

The mower blades should be sharp. A dull mower may loosen and pull at roots, and tear out grass or grass leaves. A steel file can be used to sharpen dull mower blades.

Use a grass catcher to collect grass clippings. The clippings could smother young, sprouting plants and eventually build up thatch. Removing clippings with a rake will tear out and disturb plants even if done gently.

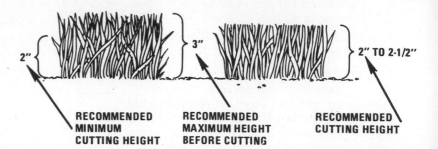

EXAMPLE:

2" — RECOMMENDED MINIMUM CUTTING HEIGHT

3" — RECOMMENDED MAXIMUM HEIGHT BEFORE CUTTING

2" TO 2-1/2" — RECOMMENDED CUTTING HEIGHT

▬ LAWN CARE ▬

▶ Watering

Watering is an important part of lawn maintenance. Plants can only benefit from the nutrients in the soil when they are in soluble form. This allows the root system to absorb them.

Many climates provide adequate water from rain most of the time. Even the best climates will not provide adequate water from rain all the time.

Hot, dry or windy periods may dry the soil deep enough to affect grass growth. In these cases, or if there is not enough rain, you will have to water your lawn. If you live in an area which provides rain in summer, do not water unless the grass shows signs of wilting. Wilting grass will turn a dull color and footprints will not disappear.

The amount of water necessary for your lawn will depend on the type of grass you have. Moisture should reach a level that encourages deep rooting of the grass. Different grasses have roots of different lengths. This is usually a minimum of 6 inches. For this reason, a thorough, deep watering is better than frequent shallow waterings.

The best time of day to water is early morning. Evening watering leaves the lawn surface damp and vulnerable to insects, disease or fungus. Early watering allows the surface to dry out before evening.

For dry climates where you have to provide water for most of the year, the following procedure will help you determine if you are watering adequately.

1. Water the area for a half-hour.

2. Dig a hole 8 to 12 inches deep.

If the hole is dark with moisture at the bottom, replace the soil and grass and water the same period of time the next week. If the bottom of the hole is dry, continue.

3. Replace the soil and grass.

4. Water the area for another half-hour.

5. Dig a hole 8 to 12 inches deep in a different spot from that dug in Step 2.

If the bottom of the hole is dry, repeat Steps 3 to 5 until bottom of hole is dark with moisture. Replace soil and grass in the last hole. The next week, water the length of time determined in the test above.

Different soils take up water at different rates. To prevent puddles or run-off of water, you may have to turn off water, wait until water is absorbed into the soil, and turn on the water again to fill the time requirement for deep watering.

▶ **Fertilizing**

Even new lawns may require fertilizing. Fertilizing will increase the height of new grass and help it to spread. New lawns should be treated with a light application of nitrogenous fertilizer every 2–4 weeks during the first growing season. Examples of nitrogenous fertilizers are ammonium sulfate, ammonium nitrate or urea.

Most spreaders have a setting for light feeding. For new lawns, use half the recommended rate on the package. The basic nutrient required for established lawns, at least once each year, is nitrogen. It is preferable to provide nitrogen several times during the year.

Fertilizer packages have a series of numbers under their name, such as 10-5-5. The first number is the percentage of nitrogen; the second, phosphorus; and the third, potassium.

Nitrogen, liquid or dry, comes in many forms and this determines if it is quick-releasing or slow-releasing fertilizer.

Organic fertilizers release nitrogen slowly to provide nitrogen over a long period of time. For these reasons, they will not "burn" the lawn.

Inorganic fertilizers are quick-acting and care must be used to prevent "burning" the lawn. Follow package directions carefully.

Fertilizers come packaged alone or in combination with insecticides or weed killer or both.

Feed cool-season grasses in the spring and fall when they are beginning their growth cycle. Warm-season grasses should be fed at the beginning of the summer months since they begin their peak growth during hot weather. Warm-season grasses can also be fed with a nitrate in the fall to promote a longer "green time" before winter dormancy.

Another indication of when to feed the lawn is if it starts to lose its color. Some soils are poor in nitrogen and the lawn will require more feeding. A strong and healthy lawn will resist wear, disease and weeds better than a lawn in distress from lack of proper nutrients.

Fertilizer can be applied using spreaders or with a liquid dispenser which attaches to a hose. Apply at the rates given on the package.

▶ **Cutting, Edging and Rolling**

The height at which to cut the grass depends on the type of grass you have and the time of the year. If you are in doubt about the type of grass you have, take a sample of your grass to your local nursery or garden shop and ask to have the type identified. Recommended normal cutting heights for different grasses are given in the section on Selecting Grasses, Page 24.

In mid-summer or very hot weather, grass should be allowed to grow 1/2 to 1 inch higher than the normal recommended cutting height. This shades the soil to keep it cool and moist. It also discourages weed seeds from germinating.

At other times of the year, grass should be mowed frequently to keep the amount of foliage removed at a minimum. If grass is allowed to grow to twice its recommended cutting height, mowing removes half of the foliage. This causes a weakened condition while the plants recover. During this time, the lawn is susceptible to attack by disease and insects. Also, it is a lot easier to mow frequently and cut off a little than to mow infrequently and fight to push the mower through a lot of top growth.

The lawn mower blades should be sharp enough to cut the grass cleanly without damaging the leaves or pulling at the roots. A dull mower bruises the ends of the grass and leaves a brown appearance on the lawn. This also leaves the lawn in an unhealthy state while it recovers from the bruises.

Lawns may be cut with hand propelled reel-type mowers or with gasoline or electrically powered mowers. Reel-type mowers are best because the grass is cut with a scissors action. This makes a clean cut on the grass blades with little bruising. Reel mowers should have at least 5 blades, and preferably 7 blades. Fewer blades result in a wavey or bumpy appearance on a newly mowed lawn.

Rotary-type mowers are powered by gasoline engines, batteries or electrical current. The cutting action is provided by a spinning blade. This does not provide as clean a cut as the reel mower. The blades require frequent sharpening for best performance. This can be done with a steel file.

WARNING

Be sure the motor is disconnected before removing the blade for sharpening.

Cutting, Edging and Rolling

When you cut or mow the lawn, start down the center and make larger and larger rectangles [1]. Using this method makes the job easier because of gradual turns. This method leaves a better-appearing lawn. Back and forth mowing tends to leave a banded appearance on the lawn.

To prevent the grass from being rolled in one direction, alternate the starting point each time you mow [2].

Grass clippings should be removed from the lawn using a grass catcher or rake. In the past, gardening experts felt that clippings should be returned to the soil to provide organic matter. The modern thought is that clippings harbor disease and insects and builds up thatch which will eventually have to be removed.

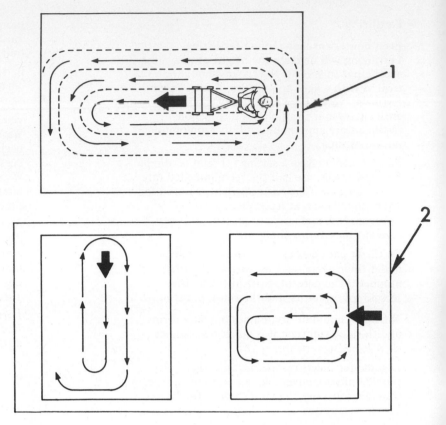

Cutting, Edging and Rolling

Edging is not necessary to maintain a healthy lawn. Edging is done to maintain a neat appearance or to keep lawns from spreading into adjacent flower beds. It is not necessary to edge each time you mow.

Requirements for edging can be reduced by using thin strips [1] of metal or plastic designed for this purpose. The strips are pushed into the soil so that they extend only 1 inch above the surface. The strips contain the grass roots and keep them from spreading into plant beds or other areas.

Mowing strips [2] can also save edging by hand. Mowing strips are bricks, stones or a narrow concrete path placed level with the soil. One wheel of the lawn mower is placed on the mowing strip and the grass along the edge is cut by mowing.

Cutting, Edging and Rolling

There are many types of long-handled edgers designed to make cutting and trimming easier. They are available in powered and un-powered models.

Edging can also be done with a hand-operated grass clipper or an electric grass clipper.

Many people feel lawns should be rolled every spring to smooth out areas pushed up by freezing and thawing. Modern thought is that rolling creates problems by compacting the soil too much. If you feel you must roll the lawn in the spring, wait until after freezing periods are over. Use a light roller which is empty or one-quarter full of water.

▶ **Controlling Insects, Diseases and Weeds**

The simplest approach to diagnosing trouble in a lawn is to take the easiest steps to correct deficiencies first and then wait to see if the lawn improves. You will find that the most common problems are the simplest to correct. If the simple steps do not correct the trouble, you must progress to resolving the more rare problem of disease.

First, ask yourself if the lawn has been receiving proper watering and nutrients. If not, apply fertilizer, water thoroughly and see if the lawn shows signs of recovery in two or three weeks. Most lawn problems are solved with this simple step. A healthy lawn will resist or recover from most troubles.

If the lawn does not appear to improve in two to three weeks, apply a commercially available insecticide containing sevin or diazinon. These two chemicals will kill any insects that may be damaging the grass blades or roots. Sevin and diazinon are recommended because they break down in the soil and do not cause indirect environmental damage, as do DDT, chlordane and others.

Insecticides are available in dry granules or in liquid form. Dry granules can be applied with a spreader as described for seeding a lawn, Page 31. Liquid insecticides are applied with a spraying bottle attached to your hose.

CAUTION

Follow label directions carefully. Do not apply insecticides on a windy day, while you are smoking or near foodstuffs. Thoroughly wash all equipment after using and do not smoke, eat or drink until you have washed your face and hands.

Store all chemicals and equipment away from children and pets. If chemicals spill on your skin or clothing, wash immediately with soap and water.

If you still see no improvement after two or three weeks, the problem is probably a disease and fungicide must be applied.

Controlling Insects, Diseases and Weeds

Fungicides usually come in liquid form to be sprayed over the lawn area. Since rain or watering wash off the active ingredients, an additional application of the fungicide is usually applied a week later. With a persistent fungus, additional applications may be needed and applied a week apart.

Select a general fungicide that is effective on the greatest number of diseases. This information is found on the label.

Your garden supply dealer might be able to suggest an all-purpose fungicide that seems to be effective on the diseases that affect your area.

CAUTION

Follow label directions carefully. Do not apply fungicides on a windy day, while you are smoking or near foodstuffs. Thoroughly wash all equipment after using and do not smoke, eat or drink until you have washed your face and hands.

Store all chemicals and equipment away from children and pets. If chemicals spill on your skin or clothing, wash immediately with soap and water.

Controlling Insects, Diseases and Weeds

The best way to control weeds in a lawn is to keep it properly fed and watered. A thick turf will keep out most weeds and the few that do grow can be removed by hand. This will eliminate purchasing and storing dangerous chemical weed killers.

However, if weeds are already a problem in the lawn, there are many effective and convenient-to-use chemicals available.

Weeds fall into two groups. One group is the grassy weeds [1] such as crab grass or foxtail. The other group of weeds are called broad-leaf weeds [2], such as plantain or chickweed.

Entirely different chemicals are used to treat the grassy and broad-leafed weeds. Great care must be used during application of these chemicals to prevent damage to other plants in the yard.

If you have a serious infestation of weeds in a lawn, it is suggested you take a few of the weeds to your local nursery or garden supply store. They can suggest what seems to work best in your area and tell you exactly what weeds you are dealing with. Be sure you know what kind of grass your lawn is. If you are not sure, take along a sample.

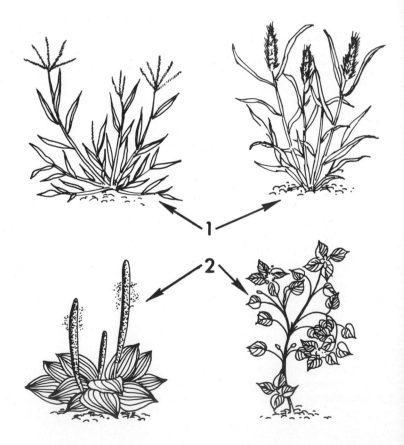

Controlling Insects, Diseases and Weeds

Weed-killing chemicals are available in several forms:

- Aerosol foam [1]
- Liquid to be mixed with water and applied with a wand [2] or spraying bottle [3].
- Impregnated wax bar [4] that is dragged across the lawn
- Dry chemicals that are spread over the entire lawn as for fertilizing or seeding.

Do not apply weed killers with a sprayer on a windy day as they could drift in the wind to valuable plants in your yard or your neighbor's yard.

Do not use weed-killing equipment such as sprayers or watering cans for fertilizing or insecticides. The traces of chemicals in the containers could injure plants or lawns.

Always follow package directions carefully. Mixing a solution stronger to do a better job does not work. Many chemicals will then injure the lawn.

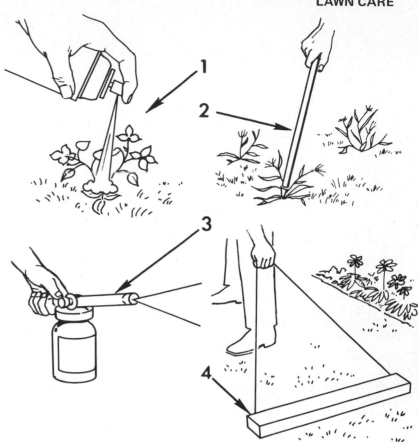

RENOVATING A LAWN

▶ Preparations for Renovating

Replanting a lawn is quite a large task. It is more work than putting in the original lawn because you must first remove the old lawn. Therefore, consider it only as a last resort. Usually, renovation will restore a lawn with a lot less work.

To improve a poor lawn, you must first determine the cause of the problem. The answer could be simple neglect. Beginning a program of proper maintenance may produce a healthy, thriving lawn.

If you have inherited a lawn from a previous owner, check to make sure the grass is right for your area. Perhaps there is too much shade for the grass that is there. If so you must change the grass or remove the cause of the shade. Some of these questions could be discussed with your

local nursery. Take a sample of the grass with you.

Read the sections on Aerating, Page 44, and Dethatching, Page 45. Examine the lawn to determine whether aerating or dethatching is necessary. If so, aerate or dethatch the lawn as required.

After taking the required renovating steps, start a vigorous maintenance program. Proper maintenance will restore the lawn and prevent future problems.

If the above procedures do not revitalize the lawn, more drastic action may be required. This could require replanting a section of the lawn.

RENOVATING A LAWN

▶ Aerating

Aerating is a method used to open up compacted soil. When soil is compacted, water runs off the surface and does not penetrate deeply. The grass roots do not receive water, oxygen or nutrients.

Compacted soil is indicated when the lawn develops hard, bare spots, dry spots, or areas of crabgrass or knotweed. Digging up a spade-size piece of lawn will allow you to determine if there is a compacted layer of soil near the surface.

Compacted soil is caused by heavy traffic, using a roller that is too heavy, rolling too frequently, or a high level of clay in the soil. If the soil has too much clay, it will be necessary to add organic matter to cure the problem.

Aerating can be accomplished using an aeri-fork [1] or an aerating machine [2]. Aerating tools are designed to remove small plugs of compacted soil to allow penetration of water and nutrients.

An aerating machine can be rented at equipment rental agencies, garden supply stores or nurseries. If renting an aerating machine, be sure to have the salesman show you how to start and operate the machine.

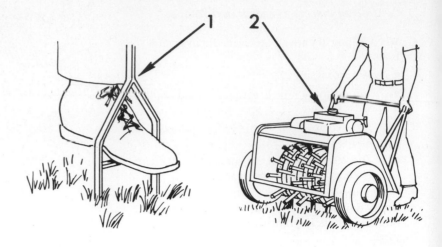

Do not use a garden fork to make holes in lawn. This method further compacts the soil behind the fork tines.

Aerating

1. Using foot pressure on an aeri-fork or using an aerating machine, remove plugs of soil from entire lawn area. If using aeri-fork, space holes about 6 inches apart.

2. Using back of rake or drawing a length of chain link fencing [1], break up the plugs.

3. Using rake, remove any pieces of loose grass or roots.

4. Spread a 1/2-inch layer of organic matter over the area.

5. Using back of rake, force loose soil and organic matter into the holes [2] left by aerating.

6. Spread fertilizer over the area.

7. Water lawn thoroughly. Water at least once a week for 3 to 4 weeks.

44

▶ Dethatching

Thatch [1] is the build-up of grass clippings and undecomposed leaves on the surface of the soil. A little thatch is beneficial in that it shades and cools the soil.

However, a layer of thatch that is thicker than 3/4 of an inch prevents water, nutrients and oxygen from reaching the grass roots.

If the lawn has dry or dead patches and feels springy when you walk on it, check for thatch. Digging up a small portion will help you determine the thickness of the layer of thatch.

Dethatching can be accomplished using a bladed rake [2] or a dethatching machine [3]. The dethatching machine can be rented at most garden supply stores, equipment rental agencies or nurseries. The machine is the preferred method of dethatching because it disturbs the grass roots less than the rake.

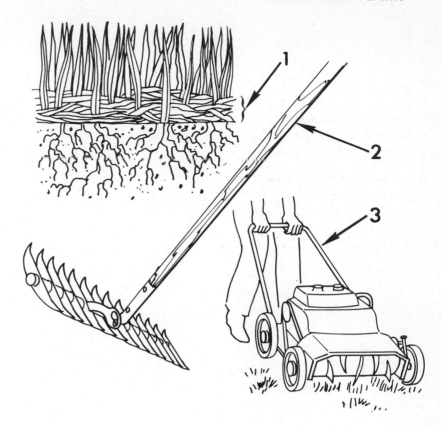

Dethatching

If using a dethatching machine, be sure to have the salesman show you how to start and operate it. Try to rent a heavy-duty model.

1. Using dethatching machine [1] or pulling a rake toward you [2], cut through the lawn. This will cut through the thatch and bring it to the surface.

2. Using a leaf rake, rake up and remove thatch. If you have a large lawn, have people to help remove the thatch. You will be amazed by how much thatch must be removed.

3. Mow the lawn using a lawn mower with a grass catcher. This will cut off straggly stems and smooth the lawn.

4. Spread fertilizer over lawn area.

5. Water fertilizer into the lawn. Water at least once a week for 3 or 4 weeks.

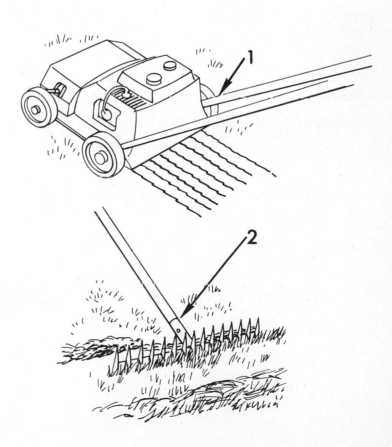

▶ **Replacing Damaged Areas**

Some bare spots in a lawn may be too large for a revitalized lawn to spread and cover. Replant large bare spots using seed or plugs cut from healthy parts of the lawn.

When cutting plugs from other parts of the lawn, make straight, deep cuts to remove as much of the root system as possible.

See Planting a Lawn, Page 26, to prepare the soil for planting.

The soil should be made level with the surrounding area. Add or remove soil as required.

GROUND COVERS

Low-growing plants from 3 inches high to 3 feet high can be used in place of grasses as ground cover. Examples of such plants are ivy, flowering bushes and evergreen plants such as juniper. Additional examples, along with criteria to help you select a ground cover, appear later in this section.

Ground covers are selected for appearance. They are also selected to solve yard problems. Some ground covers will grow in very shady spots where grass will not grow. Ground covers are a good choice for slopes which are hard to mow or for steep slopes to prevent erosion.

Some ground covers will accept adverse soil conditions in which grass will not do well. However, it is best to select the ground covers that grow well in your type of soil rather than to change the soil to suit the plant.

Since the choice of ground cover plants throughout the country is wide, it is desirable to visit your local nursery. There you can determine the plants that do well in the climate and soil conditions in your area.

Before you visit the nursery, know the places you want to use the ground cover and describe those to the nurseryman. Information commonly needed is the size of the location, whether the soil is very wet or very dry, amount of sun or shade, and if traffic across the area is required.

You will want to know the size of the plants at maturity to prevent constant cutting back of plants that are too large for the chosen spot. Check the tables that follow or ask your nurseryman.

The nursery should have growing samples of plants that do well in your area and information as to how many to buy to cover the ground in one year.

The following pages present typical ground covers and some of the criteria for selection.

GROUND COVERS THAT TOLERATE COLD, MODERATE AND WARM CLIMATES				
MATURE HEIGHT	GROUND COVER	COLORS	SOIL PREFERENCE	SUN-SHADE PREFERENCE
3"	Ground Ivy	light to deep green foilage	any	either
	Moss Sandwort*	white flower	requires very fertile soil	partial shade
10"	Bearberry*	dark green leaf bright red fruit	acid sandy	sun
24"	Crownvetch**	pink flower	any	sun
	Juniper***	light green to blue foilage	any	sun
36"	Coralberry	red berries	any	full sun to partial shade

    * Tolerates colder climates of Montana, North Dakota and Northern Minnesota
  ** Not recommended for warm climates
*** Also does well in sub-tropic climate regions

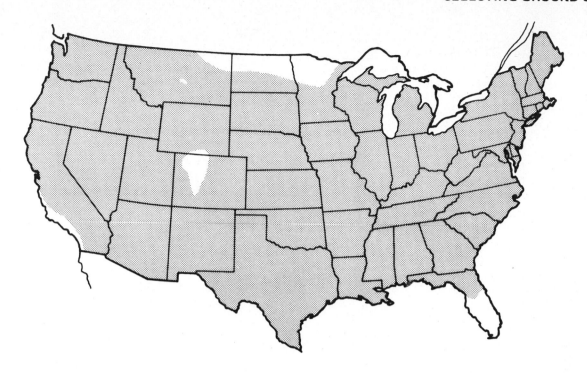

COLD, MODERATE AND WARM CLIMATE REGIONS

MATURE HEIGHT	GROUND COVER	COLORS	SOIL PREFERENCE	SUN – SHADE PREFERENCE
	GROUND COVERS THAT TOLERATE MODERATE AND WARM CLIMATES			
3″	Creeping Thyme*	evergreen purple flower	dry	full sun
	Periwinkle*	evergreen white to purple flower	any	sun or partial shade
	Wintergreen**	white flowers red berries	acid moist	shade
8″	Bugleweed	blue to purple flower	any	either
	English Ivy*	shades of green	any	either
	Honeysuckle	evergreen white or yellow flowers	any	either
12″	Barrenwort,** ***	white, yellow or lavender flowers	any	semi-shade
	Cowberry	pink flowers dark red berries	acid	partial shade
	Creeping Lilyturf*	dark green leaf purple flower	any	either
	Heartleaf Bergania*	pink flowers in May	any	either
	Memorial Rose	semi-evergreen white flowers	sandy	sun
24″ – 30″	Cotoneaster*	white or pink flowers bright red berries	any	full sun
	Dwarf Polyganium,* ***	foliage is red in summer	rocky or gravel	full sun

*   Also does well in sub-tropic climate regions
**   Not recommended for warm climates
*** Tolerates cooler regions just north of the moderate climate regions

SELECTING GROUND COVERS

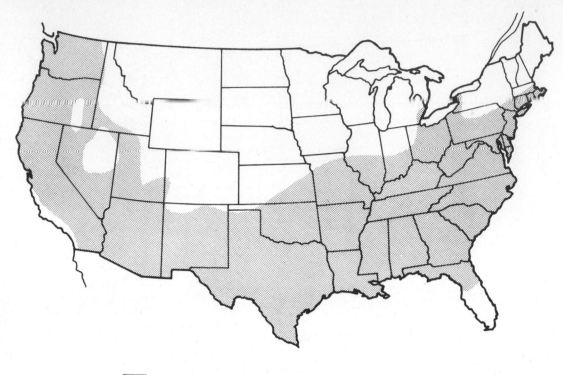

☐ MODERATE AND WARM CLIMATE REGIONS

GROUND COVERS THAT TOLERATE ONLY WARM CLIMATES				
MATURE HEIGHT	GROUND COVER	COLORS	SOIL PREFERENCE	SUN – SHADE PREFERENCE
4"	Capeweed*	greenish purple leaf light pink flower	sandy	either
9"	Iceplant**	brilliant colors in full sun	any	full sun
	South African Daisy*	light green leaf orange flowers	any	sun
	Wandering Jew**	striped leaves — green and white or green and purple	any	shade
12"	Dwarf Hollygrape	evergreen yellow flower	any	either
	Dwarf Lilyturf***	dark green leaf purple flower	any	either
	Germander****	shades of rose to lavender flowers	any	either
	St. Johnswort****	yellow flowers	sandy	semi-shade
	Strawberry Geranium***	small white flowers	any	partial shade
24" – 72"	Japanese Holly****	green foliage	any	sun or semi-shade
	Saracocca (up to 72")****	white flowers	any	shade
	Weeping Latana***	wide range of colors	any	sun

*   Recommended for very warm and sub-tropic climate regions only
**   Limit to sub-tropic climate regions only
***   Does best in very warm and sub-tropic climate regions
****   Also does well in sub-tropic climate regions

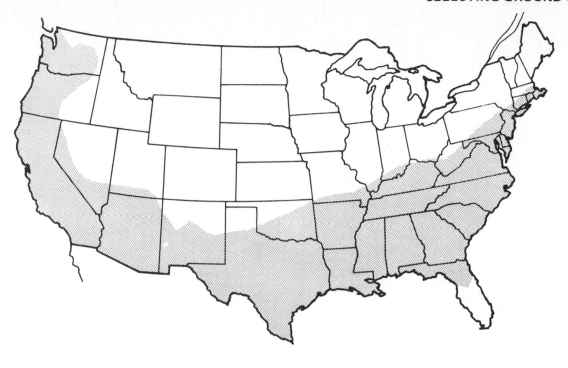

☐ **WARM CLIMATE REGIONS**

■■ **PLANTING GROUND COVERS** ────────────

▶ **Preparing the Site**

How the site is prepared for your ground cover depends largely on the type of plant you choose and the slope of the area to be planted.

Remember that the condition of the soil is a factor in your selection and that any deficiencies should be corrected before planting. As discussed earlier, it is better to select ground covers that grow well in your type of soil rather than change the soil to suit the plant. Soil conditions and corrective procedures are described in Soil Conditions, Page 8.

Ground covers can be purchased in several different forms.

- Seeds
- Flats
- Pots
- One-gallon cans or larger

The following page describes specific site preparation requirements for ground covers purchased in each of these forms.

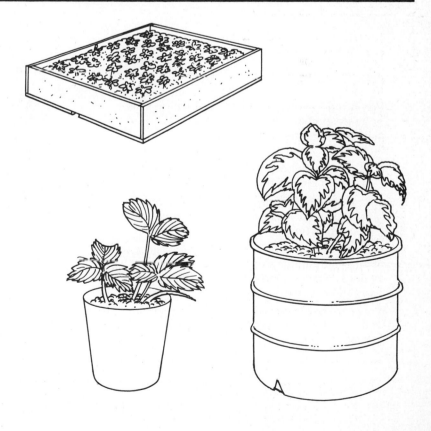

Preparing the Site

For ground covers planted as seeds, or for those which are planted from flats or pots, the site is prepared following the same procedures as preparing sites for lawns, Page 26. However, it is important to remember the following points:

- Be sure to keep plants in flats or pots moist until planting time.

- On steep slopes, till the soil with a spade. The rotary tiller can be hard to handle and dangerous on steep slopes.

- When raking soil smooth on slopes, work from the bottom to the top of the slope. This prevents thinning the soil at the top and pulling it to the bottom.

Preparing the Site

For ground covers planted from 1-gallon cans or larger, prepare the site the same as for planting trees and shrubs, Page 62. It is important to remember the following points:

- Be sure to keep plants in cans moist until planting time.

- Holes are spaced according to the recommendations for the ground cover you are planting.

Before planting your ground cover, consider correcting undesirable slopes in the area to be planted. Several methods of providing level areas and keeping the soil in place are shown.

On steep banks, consider installing a retaining wall. Gentle slopes generally require no special handling.

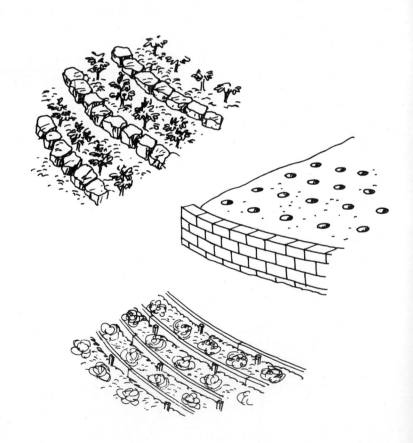

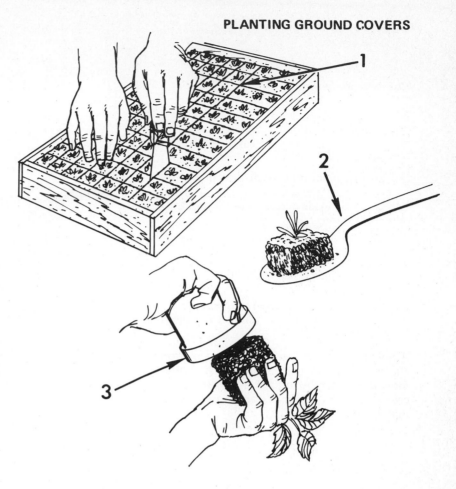

▶ Methods of Planting

Removing plants from a flat or pot requires special care to prevent damaging the plant or its root systems.

Plants are removed from a flat as follows:

1. Gently tap sides and bottom of flat to loosen soil.

2. Using a putty knife or spatula, make cuts [1] between plants.

3. Using a garden trowel or large spoon [2], gently lift out plant, disturbing roots as little as possible. Remove only one plant at a time.

Plants are removed from a pot as follows:

1. Gently tap sides and bottoms of pot to loosen soil.

2. Tip pot [3] into hand and gently pull off pot. Do *not* pull plants out of pot.

Methods of Planting

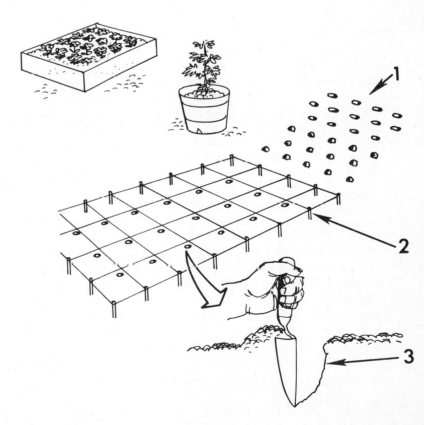

The following instructions apply to planting ground covers from flats or pots. Read through entire procedure before beginning.

If planting from seeds, ground cover is planted using instructions for planting grass seed, Page 30. If planting from 1-gallon cans or larger, ground cover is planted using instructions for planting trees and shrubs, Page 63.

Spacing between plants should be according to the recommendations for the specific ground cover you are planting.

On slopes, planting in staggered rows [1] will help prevent rain or water from washing away soil and plants.

1. Using stakes and strings [2] or small stones, mark planting positions.

2. Using garden trowel or a large spoon, make holes [3] for each plant. Holes must be larger and slightly deeper than the root system of the plant.

PLANTING GROUND COVERS

Methods of Planting

3. Gently place plant in hole [1] so it is slightly lower than surrounding soil. This acts as a basin to catch and hold water.

Soil around plant must be at the same level on the stem as it was when in the flat or pot. Banks can be made across gentle slopes to help hold water.

4. Using your hands, firm soil [2] around the plant.

5. Repeat Steps 3 and 4 to plant all ground cover.

Each plant must be watered individually. Water gently to prevent washing away the soil around the plant.

A mulch should be spread over the soil around and between each plant. The mulch retains moisture, cools the soil and helps prevent weed growth. Ask your nursery about the type of mulch to use.

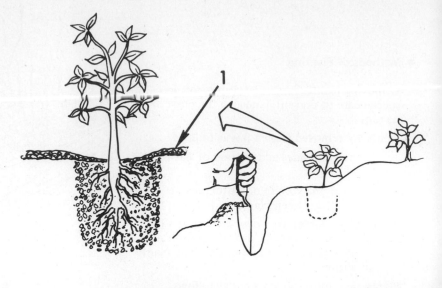

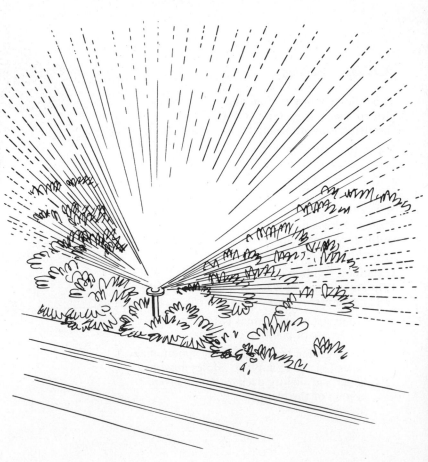

▶ **Watering New Ground Cover**

The newly planted area must be kept moist, but not wet, until the roots are established and plants show new growth. In some localities, this may mean frequent watering for 4 to 8 weeks.

Wait for the surface of the area to dry out and become light in color before watering. Then water enough to evenly darken the planting area. If the soil is kept too wet, problems with disease or insects can result.

Watering may be done by hand or with a portable or permanently installed sprinkling system. Sprinklers should be at least 3 or 4 inches higher than the height of the plants to assure even distribution of water.

If you have planted ground cover from seed, follow the watering procedure for seeds, Page 33.

Water should fall on the area in a spray or fine mist. Water should not:

•   Wash across the area, causing soil to wash away from seeds or plant roots.

•   Splash the soil from the seeds or roots.

•   Form puddles.

▶ Watering

Ground covers require regular watering to maintain healthy growth. During hot, dry or windy weather, or if you live in an area that does not provide enough rain, you will have to provide water.

Water when plants show signs of lack of moisture. Leaves of the plants will start to wilt, change color, and branches or stems will lose flexibility when the plant needs water.

If you live in an area where you must provide water on a regular basis, avoid frequent, shallow watering. The soil must be moist to a depth of 6 to 8 inches to encourage deep root development.

A simple method of determining how deeply you are watering is described on Page 38.

Do not water plants when temperatures are below freezing.

Some ground covers need protection in the winter. Plants are not injured by the cold, but by thawing and then refreezing. A blanket of snow is the best protection for plants.

If weather is below freezing without snow, cover the plants with evergreen branches or burlap. *Do not cover* before temperatures reach freezing, and do not remove the cover until temperatures remain above freezing in the spring.

▶ Fertilizing

Ground covers do not have the same fertilizing requirements as lawns.

An application of all-purpose fertilizer in the spring is usually sufficient. Choose the dry granule or pellet form. Apply as directed on the package. Scatter the granules evenly over the plants on a day when the leaves of the plants are thoroughly dry. Water the fertilizer into the soil thoroughly and be sure there are no granules remaining on any leaves. This could cause a chemical burn to the foliage.

In the western part of the country where the soil contains lime, ground cover plants may show a lack of iron. This condition is known as iron chlorosis. The leaves of the plants look pale green, yellow or almost white between the veins. The veins usually remain green. Evergreen plants will look a yellow-green rather than the normal dark green.

The most effective remedy for iron chlorosis is to apply iron in chelate form. This form reaches the plant faster.

Iron chelates come in forms to be diluted in water and applied to the foliage with a spray attachment to your hose or in forms to be mixed into the soil.

Follow package directions carefully. Do not mix solutions on concrete sidewalks or driveways. Any spilled solution will leave a permanent red stain.

MAINTAINING GROUND COVERS

▶ **Trimming**

Different types of ground covers have different trimming requirements. Some plants benefit from severe trimming and others do better if left alone. Your nursery can tell you whether your ground cover should be trimmed or not.

Some plants grow so fast that occasional trimming is required throughout the year to keep them in bounds. Others may only require trimming once a year.

Other reasons for cutting and trimming ground covers are as follows:

• To make plants bushier or to develop thicker foliage.

• To make plants uniform in appearance.

• To reduce the size of some plants to harmonize with other plants.

• To keep plants growing where you want them.

• To remove damaged or diseased portions of plants. Remove damaged or diseased portions of plants as soon as possible to assist the plant in its recovery.

As different ground covers have different growth habits, they also have different preferred times for cutting and trimming. Check with your nursery about the correct time to trim.

Plants growing on slopes or having trailing branches may spread in an unwanted direction. They may grow down the slope instead of across the slope. These plants may be trimmed or the branch may be placed where desired and restrained with a wire.

Several methods and tools are needed to trim ground covers:

• Use a rotary lawn mower to trim low growing ground covers such as dichondra.

• Use a small pruning tool when trimming only a few branches.

• Use a hedge shears when trimming the surface of an entire ground cover bed.

▶ **Controlling Insects, Diseases and Weeds**

If you notice holes, spots or curled up leaves on the ground cover plants, the problem is usually insects. If you can see large insects, such as caterpillars, hand-pick them off. A strong jet of water from the hose will knock off many smaller insects. Be sure to spray both the underside and the tops of the leaves.

If the plants are still bothered by insects, spray with a liquid form of sevin or diazinon. These two chemicals will kill insects and not cause long-lasting damage to the environment.

CAUTION

Follow label directions carefully. Do not apply insecticides on a windy day, while you are smoking or near foodstuffs. Thoroughly wash all equipment after using and do not smoke, eat or drink until you have washed your face and hands.

Store all chemicals and equipment away from children and pets. If chemicals spill on your skin or clothing, wash immediately with soap and water.

Ground cover plants do not often suffer from disease. If the plants show continued damage after spraying with an insecticide, it is best to cut out the damaged portions. The damaged portions are removed to prevent infecting the healthy plants.

If you still do not notice any improvement in two or three weeks, or if damage is extensive, cut off a portion of the damaged area. Take this sample to a nursery to find out exactly what the problem is and the proper chemical treatment.

The best way to control weeds in ground cover plants is to pull them by hand. Be sure the ground is moist enough to remove the entire root system of the weed.

Since the sun must reach the weed seeds for germination, a mulch of straw, peat moss, wood chips or bark placed around the plants will prevent weeds.

TREES AND SHRUBS

Man's appreciation of trees from a landscaping standpoint involves both practical matters such as visual screening, sunshade and wind protection, and aesthetic considerations such as shape, color and texture.

The selection of trees and shrubs could encompass literally thousands of varieties, both primary and sub-strain types. However, in order to provide some practical guidance in selection, only the most popular varieties will be considered here. Basic considerations such as mature size and hardiness zones are indicated in the following tables.

TREES THAT TOLERATE VERY COLD TO SUB-TROPIC CLIMATE REGIONS				
MAXIMUM MATURE HEIGHT	TREE	(1) DECIDUOUS	(2) EVERGREEN	COMMENTS
60'	Arborvitae		x	wide application, hearty
	Yew		x	vigorous, spreading
100'	Aspen	x		needs dry, sandy soils
	Birch	x		good for accent
	Cottonwood	x		highly wind resistant
	Juniper		x	needs dry, sandy soils
	Larch	x		grows rapidly
	Willow	x		low hanging, graceful branches
130'	Ash	x		slow growth
	Butternut	x		needs rich soils, subject to diseases
	Maple	x		very useful shade tree
	Poplar	x		grows rapidly
Over 130'	Basswood	x		very useful shade tree
	Elm	x		excellent shade tree, subject to diseases
	Fir		x	very tall, slender, good wind resistance
	Oak (varieties)	x	x	slow growth, stately fall colors
	Pine		x	very useful, disease free
	Spruce		x	needs dry, sandy soils

(1) Deciduous — drops leaves in fall
(2) Evergreen — not subject to dormancy

▨ **VERY COLD TO SUB-TROPIC CLIMATE REGIONS**

TREES THAT TOLERATE COLD TO SUB-TROPIC CLIMATE REGIONS				
MAXIMUM MATURE HEIGHT	TREE	(1) DECIDUOUS	(2) EVERGREEN	COMMENTS
40′	Dogwood	x		very attractive flowering tree
	Judas-Tree	x		colorful blooms, prefers shade
	Lilac	x		small tree, brilliant flowers, disease free
60′	Alder	x		tolerates very wet soils
	Goldenrain	x		bright yellow blooms in early summer
	Hawthorn	x		sharp thorns, broad spreading tree
	Sassafras	x		excellent for windy areas
	Sourwood	x		very slow growth, brilliant fall colors
100′	Chestnut	x		prefers rich, moist soils
	Katsuma-Tree	x		bright fall colors, graceful form
	Scholartree	x		fall blooms, useful shade tree
	Sweetgum	x		bright fall colors, native to East Coast
130′	Beech	x		brilliant fall colors, stately form
	Sycamore	x		excellent shade tree
	Walnut	x		prefers rich soils, stately form
OVER 130′	Cypress (varieties)	x	x	rapid growth, requires little care
	Ginko	x		dioecious (3), needs rich soils
	Hickory	x		can tolerate very wet soils
	Linden	x		excellent shade tree
	Maidenhair	x		dioecious (3), use male species only
	Tulip-Tree	x		attractive blossoms, rapid growth

(1) Deciduous — drops leaves in fall   (3) Dioecious — exists in male and female species
(2) Evergreen — not subject to dormancy

SELECTING TREES AND SHRUBS

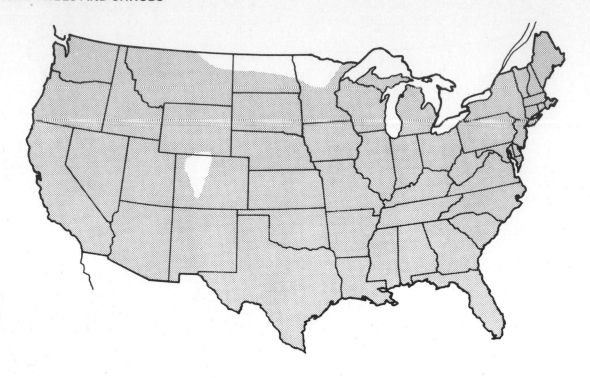

▣ COLD TO SUB-TROPIC CLIMATE REGIONS

MAXIMUM MATURE HEIGHT	TREE	(1) DECIDUOUS	(2) EVERGREEN	COMMENTS
	TREES THAT TOLERATE MODERATELY COLD TO SUB-TROPIC CLIMATE REGIONS			
40'	Olive	x	x	rapid growth, drops fruit, disease free
	Silverball	x		rapid growth, disease free
60'	Elder	x		prefers wet soils
	Fanklinia	x		very slow growth, prefers partial shade
	Holly		x	slow growth, slim shape
	Hornbeam	x		needs sandy soils, good wind resistance
	Magnolia	x		spectacular flowering, disease free
	Mulberry	x		good wind breaker
100'	Catalpa		x	very rapid growth
	Cherry	x		prefers dry, sandy soils
	Hemlock		x	needs room to spread, disease free
	Locust	x		very rapid growth, disease free
	Snowbell	x		controllable for small locations, summer flowers
130'	Bay		x	applicable to milder climates
Over 130'	Cedar		x	very hardy, graceful lines, mild climates only

(1) Deciduous — drops leaves in fall
(2) Evergreen — not subject to dormancy

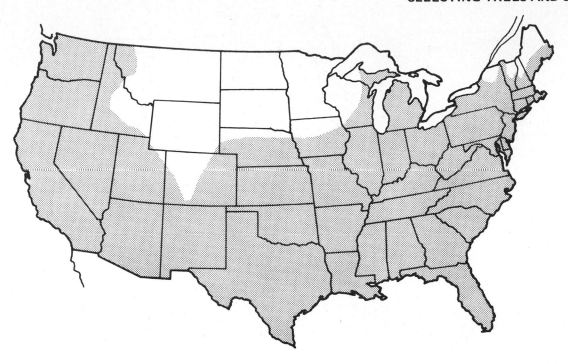

■ MODERATELY COLD TO SUB-TROPIC CLIMATE REGIONS

\multicolumn{5}{c}{SHRUBS AND CLIMATE REGIONS THEY TOLERATE}
MAP	SHRUB	COLORS	SOIL PREFERENCE	SUN — SHADE PREFERENCE
I	Hydrangea	white thru purple — July	any	either
	Juniper	evergreen	sandy	sun
	Laurel	white-pink — June	sandy, acid	shade
	Lilac	white thru lavender June — July	neutral	sun
	Viburnum	white flower, reddish fruit — April-June	wet, rich	sun
II	Azalea	white, yellow, scarlet April-July	acid	semi-shade
	Honeysuckle	white-rose — March-April	any	sun
	Ilex	white — June-July	rich	either
	Jasmine	yellow — February-March	rich	partial sun
	Rhododendron	white-purple — May	acid	shade
	Tamarisk	pink — April-September	neutral	sun
III	Barberry	yellow-bloom, red fruit April	neutral	sun
	Box	evergreen	rich	semi-shade
	Forsythia	yellow — April	any	either
	Hibiscus	white-purple — August	not too sandy	either
	Hollygrape	yellow — April	dry, sandy	shade
	Privet	white flower, black fruit July-September	any	either
IV	Abelia	white-pink — June-Nov.	any	either
	Camellia	white-deep red — October-May	good drainage	partial shade
	Pittosporum	evergreen white-yellow flower	any	either
	Pyracantha	white flower, orange red fruit — May-June	well drained	sun

SELECTING TREES AND SHRUBS

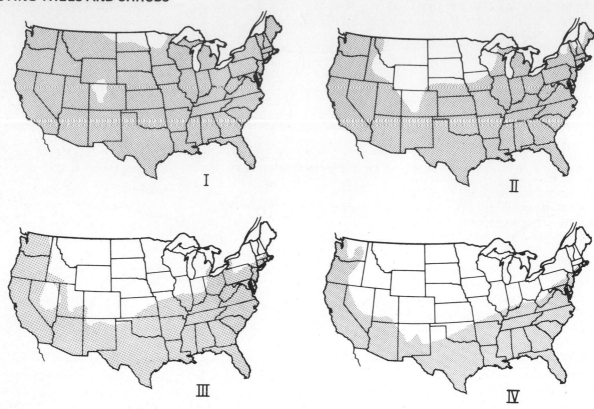

I   II

III   IV

☐ GROWTH REGIONS

━━━ PLANTING TREES AND SHRUBS

▶ Preparing the Site

Soil conditions will affect the growth and health of any trees you plant. While it is possible to effectively change some aspects of soil conditions, it is usually preferable to select trees that are more adaptable to the existing conditions.

The soil should be moist, not wet or dry, when preparing the site.

The soil should have good drainage to insure proper aeration. Improper aeration will inhibit healthy root development and encourage disease or decay.

1.   Using shovel, make hole at planting site. Make hole at least 1-1/2 times as deep and twice as wide as the root system of the plant.

2.   Mix organic material, commercially available planter's mix and soil conditioners with an equal amount of soil removed in Step 1.

3.   Using shovel or gardening fork, loosen soil at bottom of hole to a depth of 4 to 10 inches.

4.   Fill hole approximately 1/3 full using mixture prepared in Step 2.

▶ **Methods of Planting**

If root system is enclosed in a container, remove container before continuing. If the root system is wrapped in burlap [1], do not remove the wrapping.

Cut and remove any damaged roots from the plant.

1.   Place plant in hole [2]. If plant has bare roots, spread root system [3] so that roots are not cramped. If the plant has a burlap wrapping, untie and loosen the wrapping. It is not necessary to remove the wrapping.

2.   Check that root system is at a level consistent with the natural depth of planting. The depth of previously planted trees and shrubs should be noted to assure this. Bare root plants may have a distinctive change in form or shape at the soil line to indicate the natural depth.

3.   Add or remove soil beneath the roots as required to place root system [3] at the correct depth.

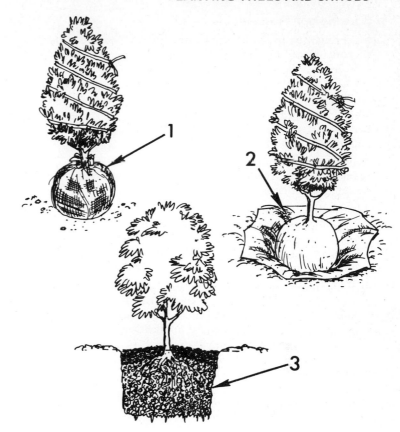

Methods of Planting

4.   Using mixture prepared from instructions on Page 62, fill hole approximately 3 inches [1].

5.   Gently press mixture into firm contact with root system.

6.   Repeat Steps 4 and 5 until the hole is filled.

7.   Make a mound around edge of hole to form a saucer-shaped basin [2] that will retain water.

8.   Water the plant. Page 64.

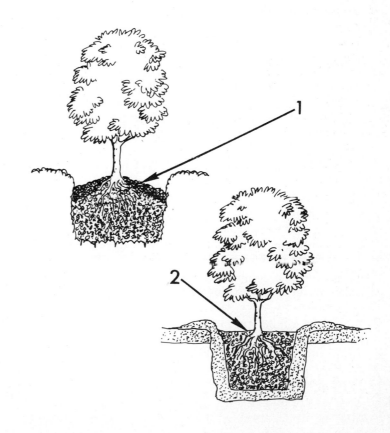

PLANTING TREES AND SHRUBS

▶ **Watering New Plantings**

Newly planted trees and shrubs must be watered thoroughly and regularly until plant is established. Watering requirements vary according to kind of plant, season and geographic area.

Watering should be thorough enough to penetrate deeply into the soil to encourage deep and healthy root development.

Keep area moist but not wet. If area is too wet, plant root system will not get enough air or will be subject to disease or decay.

Thorough watering should penetrate the full depth of the planting site, and should be repeated at intervals of 8 to 10 days. Repeat until root system is established as indicated by new growth.

Rooting hormones and vitamins are available to help the root system become established rapidly. Consult your nurseryman for advice regarding their effectiveness and application in your particular situation.

▶ **Protecting New Trees and Shrubs**

Trees or shrubs planted away from protection of buildings or walls may need to be supported in the upright position until plant is established or mature enough to withstand the effect of wind or to stay upright in soft soil caused by moisture.

It may also be necessary to protect them from loss of moisture until their root systems become established.

For instructions for protecting trees and shrubs from loss of moisture, go to Page 66.

For instructions for staking new trees and shrubs, continue.

▶ **Staking New Trees and Shrubs**

Stakes and guy wires, steel fence posts or wooden stakes may be used to support the tree or shrub.

If wooden stakes are used:

● Select cedar or redwood. They are long-lasting kinds of wood.

● Paint the part of the stake that is to be in the soil with a preservative to prevent decay.

Posts or stakes should be driven into the soil approximately 1/3 their length.

Staking New Trees and Shrubs

Plants should be tied to the stakes using stout cord or plastic-coated wires.

Ties should be threaded through plastic tubing [1] to protect plant from damage caused by ties.

Ties should be attached to the plant at 1/3 its height or higher [2].

Ties should not be tied tightly around the trunk or stem of the plant.

Ties should be tight between plant and stakes to prevent loosening of roots in soil caused by movement of the main stem or trunk.

This can be accomplished using turnbuckles or by twisting the wire loop between the plant and the stake.

Support should stay in place until plant is completely established. This could mean as long as 2 or 3 years for some plants.

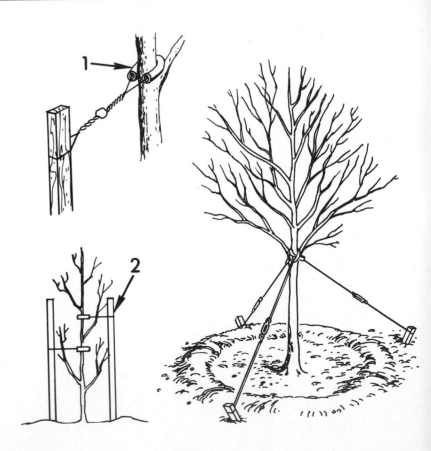

Staking New Trees and Shrubs

If the plant is less than 8 feet high and wind conditions are not severe, one stake should be adequate to support the plant:

- The stake [1] may be inside the hole used to plant the tree or shrub.
- Stake should be placed on upwind side of plant and outside of root system.

If the plant is more than 8 feet high, or if wind conditions are severe, two stakes may be required to support the plant:

- Stakes [2] should be placed so that one stake is on upwind side of plant and the other one on the downwind side.
- Both stakes may be placed inside the hole used to plant the tree or shrub but should be outside of root system.

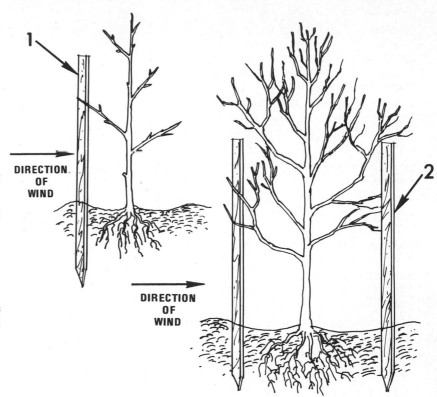

Staking New Trees and Shrubs

If winds are severe and/or from different directions, more than two stakes may be required to support the plant. Use stakes and guy wires:

- Stakes should be placed farther away from the plant, in firmer soil.
- Distance between plant and stakes should be about 1/3 of height of plant.
- One stake should be placed on the side that the predominant winds come from, and the other stakes should be spaced evenly around the plant.
- Use stakes about 1 foot long, driven about 8 inches into firm soil. Stakes should be slanted slightly away from plant.

DISTANCE IS 1/3 HEIGHT OF PLANT

▶ **Protecting New Trees and Shrubs from Loss of Moisture**

Sprays are commercially available that may be applied to foliage of newly transplanted plants to control moisture loss. Follow directions on label.

If plant has not been sprayed to prevent moisture loss, it should be pruned to remove about 1/4 of the foliage, or 1/3 of the branches and stems. Instructions for pruning begin on Page 69.

Pruning at this time gives you an opportunity to shape the new plant to your landscape plan.

Unwanted stems or branches, such as branches that cross or grow toward the center of the plant, should be removed.

If plant has damaged stems or branches, damaged parts should be cut and removed.

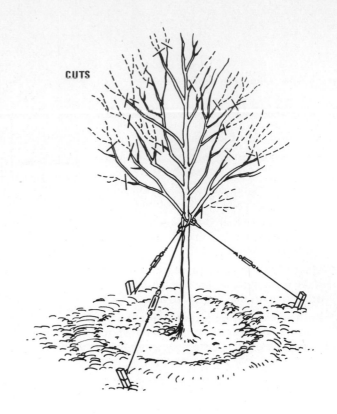

CUTS

Protecting New Trees and Shrubs from Loss of Moisture

To help soil retain moisture, and to discourage weed germination, a layer of mulch about 2 inches thick is recommended.

To reduce the possibility of disease or decay, the thickness of the mulch layer should be reduced near the trunk or main stem of the new plant.

As an alternative to using mulching material, consider planting ground covers under trees and shrubs. Ground covers thrive in varying degrees of shade and require minimum maintenance. Ground covers will serve as a living mulch for trees and shrubs.

Grass may not grow well under trees and shrubs, and if it does grow well, may be difficult to maintain.

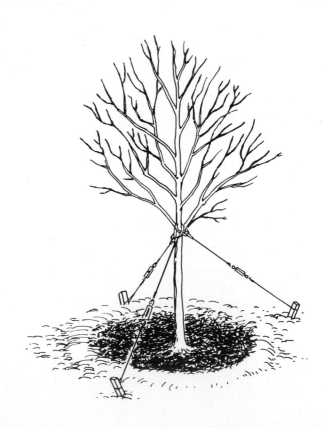

*Protecting New Trees and Shrubs
from Loss of Moisture*

Sunny and windy weather also tend to cause plant to lose moisture.

If plant has no foilage at time when planted, plant should be protected from the drying effects of sun and wind.

Protection may be accomplished by placing a wind screen or providing temporary shade for the plant.

If placing screens or shades is not practical, plant protection may be accomplished by wrapping trunk and large branches with burlap strips or durable paper.

Wrapping material should be treated with insecticide to discourage infestation during the period while the wrapping is in place.

Wrapping should stay in place at least 1 year.

MAINTAINING TREES AND SHRUBS

▶ Watering

Maintaining trees and shrubs may require watering, fertilizing and pruning or trimming.

The shallow roots of large plants in the home landscape benefit from the routine watering of the lawn, but such routine watering may not penetrate deep enough to promote development of the deep root systems.

Mature trees and large shrubs may lose many gallons of moisture during hot, dry or windy periods. This moisture can be replenished by deep watering (watering slowly for an extended time period. Water does not run off but soaks into ground). This can be done with a deep root waterer [1] or a soaker [2].

Thorough watering to permit deep penetration may be repeated at intervals of 10 days

More frequent watering may result in over-application of water. This may drown plants or promote development of disease or decay.

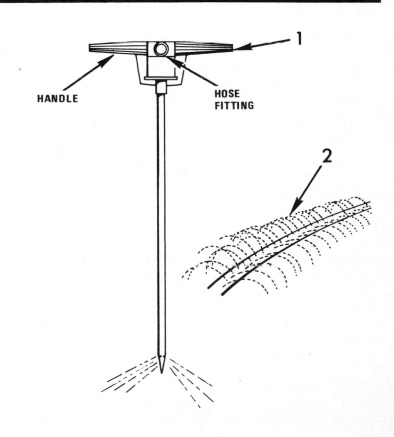

MAINTAINING TREES AND SHRUBS

▶ **Fertilizing**

Trees and shrubs require fertilizer when growth appears to be slower than normal or when foliage is paler or smaller than normal.

Fertilizer should be applied during late fall before freezing begins or in spring after freezing is over.

Do not apply fertilizers during summer or early fall. New growth, stimulated by application at this time, may not be hardy enough to survive winter conditions.

A complete fertilizer, such as 5-10-5, should be used. If using liquid or concentrated fertilizer, follow directions on label.

To fertilize trees, go to bottom of the page. To fertilize shrubs, continue.

▶ **Fertilizing Shrubs**

Use 1/2 cup of fertilizer for each small plant. Use 1 cup of fertilizer for each large plant.

Root zone spreads as far from the trunk or main stem as the spread of the branches.

1. Scatter fertilizer on top of soil evenly over the root zone.

2. Using rake, mix fertilizer with top 1/2 to 1 inch of soil.

3. Thoroughly water the area to wash fertilizer deep into the root zone.

▶ **Fertilizing Trees**

1. Using an auger or a spade, make holes [1] in soil about 1-1/2 to 2 feet deep and 1-1/2 to 2 feet apart under ends of longest branches.

2. Make holes [2] about 1-1/2 to 2 feet deep and 1-1/2 to 2 feet apart under the spread of the tree about halfway between the trunk and the holes made in Step 1.

3. Measure diameter of trunk approximately 4 feet above the ground. The diameter is approximately 1/3 of the circumference.

If diameter is less than 3 inches, use 1/2 pound of fertilizer for each inch of diameter.

If diameter is more than 3 inches, use 2 pounds of fertilizer for each inch of diameter.

The total amount of fertilizer is to be divided into equal portions so that each hole receives the same amount of fertilizer.

4. Distribute equal amounts of fertilizer to each hole [1, 2].

5. If soil was removed to make holes, fill holes with soil that was removed. Tamp soil to make it firm.

6. Thoroughly water the area to wash fertilizer deep into root zone.

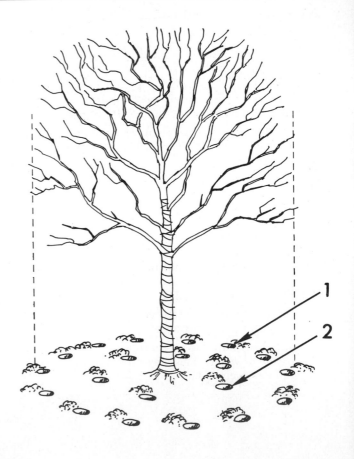

▶ **Pruning**

Pruning requirements for trees are different from the requirements for shrubs.

Trees require pruning to remove:

- Damaged, diseased or dead branches.
- Low, drooping or crossed branches.
- Branches that block out breezes or street lights.
- Branches that interfere with utility cables.
- Branches that constitute traffic hazards by obstructing views.

Shrubs require pruning to:

- Remove damaged, diseased or dead parts.
- Increase quantity or quality of blossoms or fruits.
- Improve appearance or symmetry of plants.

Springtime, before vigorous growth begins, is usually the best time for pruning.

Plants that produce blossoms or fruits should be pruned:

- In early spring before vigorous growth begins if blossoms occur on this year's growth.
- After blossoming and before fruits form if blossoms occur on last year's growth.

Careful pruning can improve the appearance and guard the health and strength of the plants.

Plants should be checked regularly for pruning needs. Pruning as soon as the need becomes evident can control small problems that would require major work if left unattended.

Small pruning cuts heal rapidly. Pruning cuts larger than 1 inch in diameter should be treated with pruning paint, grafting wax or antiseptic tree dressing to prevent entry of decay or disease as the cut heals.

For procedures for removing branches, go to next section (below).

For information for trimming trees and shrubs, go to Page 70.

▶ **Removing Branches**

Be sure cutting tools are sharp. Dull tools cause injuries that take longer to heal. When removing branch, make cut through healthy tissue, and at junction between branch and stem.

When removing small branches, make a clean cut using pruning shears.

To remove larger branches:

1. Cut *up* from the bottom [1] about 1/3 of the way through the limb out a few inches from the crotch.

2. Cut *down* from the top [2] all the way through the limb a few inches farther out from the first cut.

3. After the limb is removed, a stump will remain. Cut this stump flat to the tree trunk [3]. Healing process cannot occur properly if stub of branch remains. Bark on stub will die and permit entry of insects or disease.

4. Cover the exposed tissue at the flat cut [3] with pruning paint.

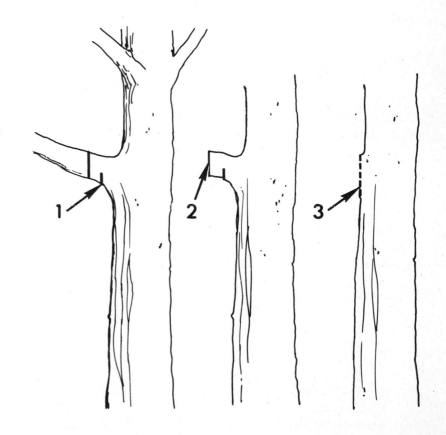

MAINTAINING TREES AND SHRUBS

▶ Trimming

Shrub-type plants try to maintain a balance between the root system development and top growth.

Removing part of the top growth will cause the plant to restore that balance with new top growth.

If top growth is pruned severely, the plant will have a strong growth reaction to produce leaf bearing shoots. This results in development of bushier top growth.

If top growth is pruned lightly, the plant will react with new growth in the buds or under-developed branches.

Pruning or trimming of plants of restricted shapes, such as hedges, may be done as required throughout the year, but most require only one or two cuttings a year.

Shrubs should be pruned in early spring, before period of vigorous growth, because new growth stimulated by pruning may not be hardy enough to survive winter conditions.

If trimming is required to keep plant in bounds, the wrong plant was selected for the location. One of three choices must be made.

- Trimming will be a routine maintenance task.
- Plant should be replaced with one with different habits.
- Chemical growth inhibitors are commercially available that retard growth to reduce trimming frequency. Check with your nurseryman about side effects. Follow instructions on label.

Go to next section (below) for making cuts.

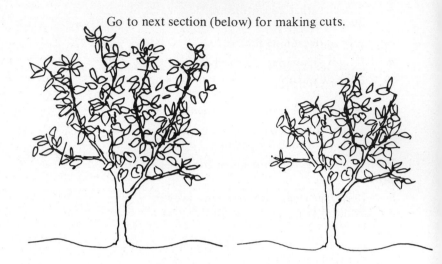

Trimming

Be sure cutting tools are sharp. Dull tools cause injuries that take longer to heal.

When removing branches, cut should be made at junction between branch and stem. Stub should also be removed, leaving a flat surface [2] on stem.

If cut is made just above a bud [1], cut should be made at slight angle to branch.

If cut is at a bud facing outward, new growth will be outward forming a spreading plant.

If cut is at a bud facing inward, new growth will be inward forming a bushier plant.

If cut is at a bud facing upward, new growth will be upward, forming a taller plant or branches that droop.

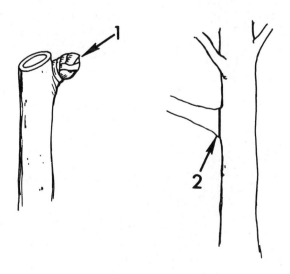

▶ Espaliering

Espaliering is a technique whereby the growth of a vine or shrub is trained to follow a specific path. Usually a trellis, wire or string is used to define the path and support the growth.

For vines or shrubs which characteristically have long thin branches, espaliering is accomplished by entwining the growth around the trellis, wire or string.

Specimens which have more woody or sturdy branches will probably require pruning or grafting to direct the growth in the manner desired. This is a much slower process, and will require a good deal of patience.

If the new growth is not sufficiently flexible to permit entwining, the growth can be secured with string or wire. Caution must be taken to avoid securing too tightly and damaging the branch as it grows and thickens. Check ties periodically and loosen if necessary.

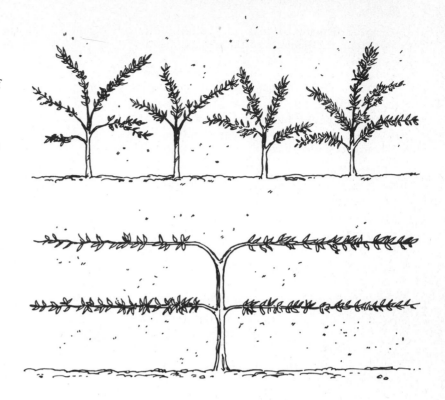

▶ Grafting

Grafting is a technique for uniting two different strains or varieties of trees or shrubs. Usually this is done to take advantage of a good root system of one, called the stock [1], and the desired growth characteristics of the other, called the scion [2].

In all cases grafting is performed in a manner such that the thin layers of growth tissue immediately beneath the bark (called the cambium) of the stock and scion are brought into direct contact with each other. This is essential to a successful graft.

Three different methods of grafting are in general use. When the stock and scion are essentially the same size in diameter, a splice graft [3] is performed. In order to firmly hold the scion and stock together a notch is sliced in each. This makes it easier to hold the two elements of the splice securely together.

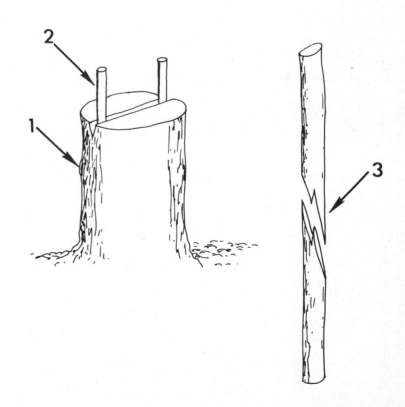

71

MAINTAINING TREES AND SHRUBS

Grafting

When the diameter of the stock is significantly larger than the diameter of the scion, either a crown graft [1] or a cleft graft [2] can be used. In both cases, as pointed out previously, the cambium of the stock and scion must be in direct contact.

In both the crown and cleft grafts it is usual to graft two scions to the stock in order to propagate symmetrically.

The crown graft [1] is made as follows:

1. Carefully split and peel back the bark of the stock.

2. Taper the bottom of the scions [3] to a point.

3. Insert the scions with the cambium of the scions in contact with the cambium of the stock.

The cleft graft [2] is made as follows:

1. Carefully split the trunk of the stock down far enough to allow the scions to be placed as shown.

2. Taper the bottom of the scions [3] to a point.

3. Insert the scions with the cambium of the scion in contact with the cambium of the stock.

When the stock and scion are mated, the jointed area should be firmly tied with clean cloth [4] and the entire mating sealed with grafting wax.

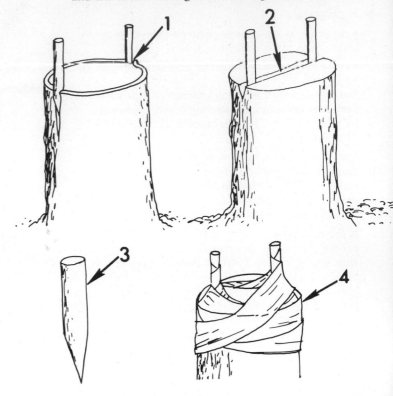

▶ Propagating

Propagating is a means of reproducing a plant. It can be accomplished in several ways.

The easiest way to propagate a new plant is through a cutting. This is a technique in which a portion of the plant is severed and planted to grow as a completely separate plant. The portion of the parent which can be cut depends upon the type of plant being propagated. Root, stem, leaf or bud cutting are among the means used to propagate, depending upon the particular plant. Your nurseryman can give you advice in this matter.

Propagation through cutting requires a good deal of attention and care. Once the cutting is severed from the parent, it must be protected from drying out. It should be planted as soon as possible to avoid exposure to anything other than its natural environment. Quite often, to increase the probability of a successful new growth, the cutting will be planted in a temporary home, such as a cutting bed [1]. In this way, careful control of the soil and its condition can be exercised. Protection from pests and diseases can be accomplished more easily in a cutting bed than in the general garden environment.

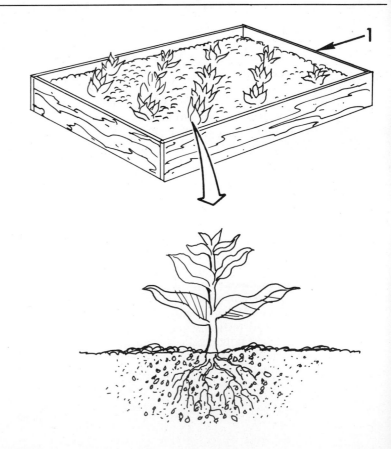

Propagating

Layering is another technique for propagation. In this case, the extremity of a branch or stem of the parent plant is cut, and a stick or pebble is placed in the cut [1]. The branch is then buried near the parent plant. This technique is particularly suited to fruiting or flowering plants. The planted tip will develop its own root system and begin to grow a second plant [2] without even being detached from the parent. After roots form, the small plant can be cut from the branch and transplanted to another location, if desired.

Certain species, such as forsythia, propagate themselves naturally by layering. Care must be taken with this type of plant to avoid unwanted growth. However, where desired, these species can be layered a number of times in a serpentine fashion from a single parent plant. Continuously expanding growth can be accomplished in this manner.

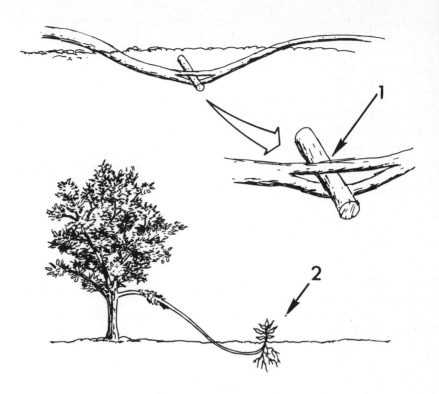

▶ Controlling Insects and Diseases

Effective control of insects or disease in trees and shrubbery begins with the recognition of a problem. To do this, one must have a basic understanding of the appearance of a healthy specimen.

In general, healthy trees, shrubs and plants should evidence no malformations, such as grossly disfigured trunks, stems, branches or top growth. Abnormal coloration on surfaces or bulbous growths are symptoms of problems. Leaves, buds or flowers which are dull in color are suspect.

Problems which affect the root growth are particularly difficult to discover and diagnose. Recognizing effects on the above-ground growth is the only way to make a determination — short of digging and exposing the roots.

The chart on Page 74 contains a listing of common tree and shrub diseases along with their symptoms and appropriate treatments.

As the case with insects, many diseases have developed an immunity to curative applications which previously were effective. Therefore, if one recommended treatment is not successful, you should try another. For this reason, the chart lists alternative treatments.

Most of the treatments (listed by their generic names, not by trade names) are available as either wettable powders or dust. The wettable powders require dilution in water. Follow the manufacturer's directions carefully in regard to the quantities of powder and water.

WARNING

Carefully note and follow the cautionary directions provided on the label of any garden spray, dust or pellet. Many of these substances are harmful to household pets or human. When spraying trees, stand back and do not let mist fall on you.

Any garden tool which comes into contact with a disease-laden tree, shrub or flower should be disinfected after use. This can be accomplished by soaking the infected tools for 1-1/2 hours in a 3% solution of hydrogen peroxide.

MAINTAINING TREES AND SHRUBS

SYMPTOM	DISEASE	TREATMENT
Lesions along veins of leaves Cankerous formations on stem	Anthracnose	Ferbam, captan
White or brown slimy spots on petals or leaves	Blight	Captan, ferbam, lime-sulphur,* maneb
Salmon-pink spore blisters on back of leaves and along stems	Canker	Benox. Remove badly cankered limbs
Spheres (up to 3 inches in diameter) on shoots or roots	Gall	Captan, cycloheximide. Remove and burn badly galled plants
Large spots (2 to 3 inches in diameter) on leaves late in season	Leaf-blotch	Ferbam, captan
Brown or grayish spots on leaves Foliage becomes disfigured	Leaf-spot	Maneb, sulphur*
White coating on foliage Dust appearance	Mildew	Ferbam, maneb, sulphur,* folpet
Lacks vigor	Rot	Ferbam, maneb. Remove badly rotted plants
Orange-yellow spots on leaves	Rust	Ferbam, sulphur,* cycloheximide
Light-brown streaks on lower leaves or limbs	Scab	Ferbam, captan. Prune badly scabbed limbs
Appears to have been in a fire	Scorch	Remove and burn
Plant suddenly wilts and dies	Wilt	Remove and burn

*Do not apply when temperature is above 85°F.

Controlling Insects and Diseases

Not all insects are harmful to your garden. Some insects known as predatory parasites are actually beneficial. These insects are the natural enemy of other insects which are damaging to garden plants. They tend to perform the same function as an insecticide in that they eliminate the damaging insect pests.

As in the case of diseases, effective control of insect pests begins with recognition. This can be accomplished in two ways — either through a recognition of the insect itself or of the damage it does.

Insect pests are grouped into two categories, depending upon the way in which they accomplish their destructiveness. One group is composed of chewing insects which attack the solid plant tissue directly. The second group is made up of sucking insects which pierce the surface of the plant tissue and suck the plant juices from within.

The damage resulting from the first group is more obvious and can usually be seen by close examination of the tree, shrub or plant. When present, these chewing insects can usually be controlled or eliminated by a stomach poison applied to the surfaces of the vegetation.

The damage resulting from sucking insects is more difficult to see until it reaches a disastrous stage. To prevent this, one must observe and recognize the insect while it is not feeding, observe the insect feeding, or recognize the symptoms in the vegetation at an early stage. Sucking-type insects are controlled through contact poisons applied directly to the skin or shell of the insect.

There are many insecticides available for you to select from. In recent years, the potentially harmful residual or side effects of numerous insecticides have been discovered. Federal, state and local agencies are continually examining this problem and provide up-to-date results to manufacturers and retailers. Your local nurseryman should be able to recommend a poison which is effective and does not cause long-lasting environmental damage.

GARDENS

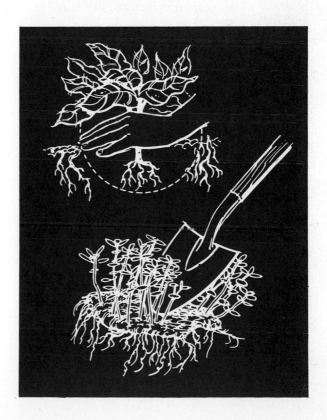

A yard made up of only lawns and trees or shrubs can be brightened up and made more attractive with gardens. The garden can be made up of perennials (permanent) and annuals (one-year life cycle).

Use gardens to tie elements of the yard and house together. Also, use gardens to prevent a "spotty" look, such as that presented by bare spots between shrubs planted next to the house.

Some common and attractive locations for gardens are:

- Under trees
- Along a fence
- Along a driveway or sidewalk
- In front of the foundations of the house
- Along edges of a patio or deck
- Along lot lines to define the yard
- Around an entry

The section on Landscaping provides information on planning the locations of garden areas.

You can use different plant types to accomplish a variety of landscaping objectives. For example:

- Use shrubs to provide privacy, as a windbreak, in foundation plants, as a screen to hide carports or service yards, or for their flowers or seasonal color. Low-growing types of shrubs may be used as a ground cover or in front of taller types of shrubs. Evergreen shrubs provide greenery in the winter.

- Use vines to soften long expanses of fencing or walls, to provide shade to a patio when grown on an overhead trellis, to soften lines of a house when trained along eaves or up porch posts or for their interesting foliage or showy flowers.

- Use annuals and perennials for ground cover between shrubs, color in the shrub border, in fence plantings or in containers to add color to a patio. Unless you are an avid gardener, do not use annuals to make up the entire garden. Mix them in with permanent plants. Quick-growing annuals provide excellent coverage of the fading foliage of bulbs.

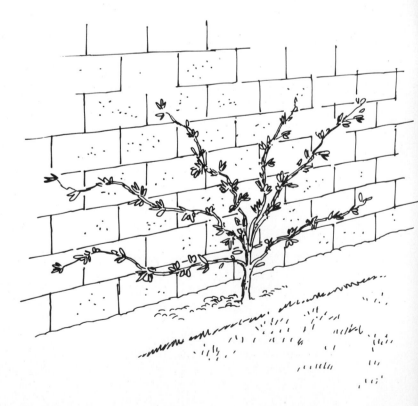

To do an effective job of planning a garden, make up a sketch of your yard, roughly to scale, on graph paper. Show existing structures and trees or shrubs you want to keep. Designate NORTH on the sketch of the yard. Indicate areas that are shaded.

Mark off the areas where gardens are desired. Each area can be done separately, such as an entry garden can be done this year and the foundation garden next year, or the entire yard can be done at once. This will depend on the amount of time and money you want to spend. However, having an overall plan will help prevent haphazard results.

After deciding where garden areas are to be, make an enlarged sketch for each separate area. Mark off designated spots for different plants as you make your selections.

Many nurseries provide a planning service in connection with the sale of plants. Your sketch will be valuable if you decide to use professional help. Make sure you see a reputable nursery that will not try to oversell plants. You could end up with a jungle and be constantly cutting plants back.

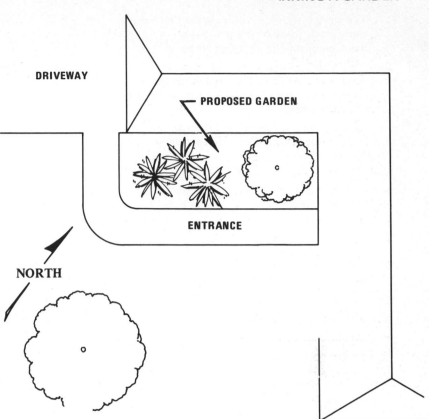

DRIVEWAY

PROPOSED GARDEN

ENTRANCE

NORTH

Plan to spend time noticing gardens in other yards in your area. If you do not have a wide knowledge of plants and their different growing needs, note which plants seem to do well and which ones you like. Also notice their exposure to sun or shade.

The nursery will have many examples of plants and usually knows which ones are best to use under local climate and soil conditions.

Use plant literature. Seed companies offer illustrated catalogues listing plant traits and new hybrids. Many nurseries have booklets on plants locally available and products to help take care of them. The public library will have garden books which list plants in encyclopedia form. Some of these books will have color illustrations of the plants.

The design of a garden requires careful planning. Consider the following ideas in your planning:

- Plants look better when two or three of the same type are grouped together, rather than placed singly.

- Decide before selecting plants whether you want a formal or informal look and select plants accordingly.

- In foundation plantings, place taller shrubs at the corners of the house or at chimneys. Don't obscure windows with plants. Bare areas between shrubs have a "finished" look if filled in with perennials, ground cover or annuals.

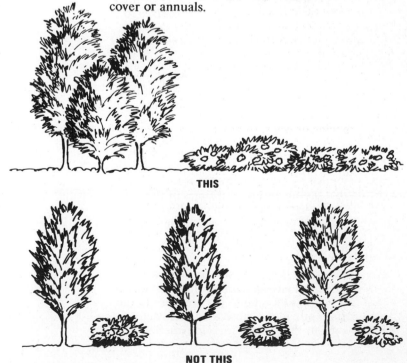

THIS

NOT THIS

PLANNING A GARDEN

- The garden shouldn't be so wide that you can't reach some of the plants for maintenance. Use stepping stones if necessary.

- Yards look better if the expanse of lawn is not broken up by "spot" planting of shrubs or other plants.

- Avoid dangerous situations such as tall hedges along a driveway or creating a "blind" corner.

- Plant flowers in curved drifts or masses. If one edge must be straight because of a driveway or sidewalk, make the other edge [1] a curve. An exception to this is in a very formal garden.

- Plant taller varieties in back along fences or walls. Group medium plants in the center and low-growing types as a border in front. Plant clumps of medium-sized plants in the background and the foreground to break the monotony [2].

- Color is important when using flowers. A mass of one color looks better than a single row. Blend shades of orange and yellow, red and pink, pink and purple. Or use colors that contrast sharply, such as yellow and blue. White can be used with any color combination.

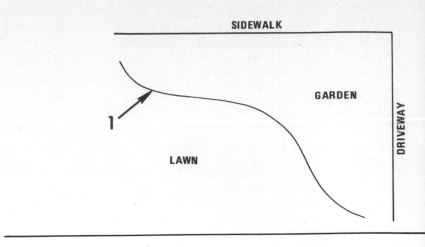

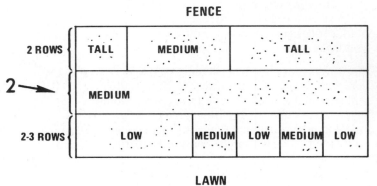

Your selection of the individual plants to make up the garden should be guided by your personal taste and the amount of time available for maintenance.

For a formal look, choose plants that grow in a column shape or those that lend themselves to pruning, such as hedges. Plants with a stiff and definite shape lend themselves to formal gardens.

For informal gardens, choose free-branching or drooping plants with a soft look. Plants that move or rustle in the wind also have an informal appeal.

For low-maintenance gardens, plan to use perennials and ground cover with perhaps a few bulbs to provide color. Include flowering shrubs in a perennial planting to provide color. Select plants that bloom at different times of the year to have color in the garden almost all year-round. Choose plants that re-seed themselves.

Select plants or hedges that grow slowly and require only annual pruning.

Plant greens and flowering shrubs first, then space annuals in among them so they will not be missed when not blooming. The greenery in the background provides a showcase for flowers. Select annuals that bloom for a long period of time.

If you enjoy spending a lot of time in the garden, large areas of annuals provide brilliant color and the enjoyment of experimenting with color combinations. Include consideration of spring, summer and fall blooming plants in your planning. In mild-winter areas, winter blooming plants should be included.

Soil conditions should be determined before selecting plants. Select plants that do well in local soil conditions and in the spot you want to place them. Other factors for you to consider are whether locations are sunny, shady, wet or dry.

Make a notebook on any special culture requirements when making plant selections, such as the needs for digging up bulbs in the fall. Incorporate this information into a maintenance schedule for the garden. This will also give you an idea in advance of the maintenance required. As a result, you may want to make changes in the selection of some of the plants.

The following charts list some of the more popular flowers. They are grouped as either annuals or perennials to aid in your selection.

FLOWERING ANNUALS			
COMMON NAME	TIME OF BLOOM	MAXIMUM HEIGHT	COLORS
Ageratum	summer	1 ft.	white, pink, blue
Baby's Breath	spring	3 ft.	white only
Bachelor's Buttons	spring — summer	2-1/2 ft.	blue
Calendula	spring — summer	2 ft.	yellow through orange
Carnation*	summer	3 ft.	white, pink through red
Cosmos	autumn	6 to 8 ft.	white, pink, lavender, crimson
Delphinium	spring — autumn	3 ft.	white, yellow, pink, red through blue
Lobelia	summer	6 in.	blue, purple
Marigold	summer	1 ft.	yellow through red
Nasturtium	spring — autumn	6 ft.	pink through mahogany
Pansy	winter — spring	9 in.	white, yellow, red, blue
Petunia	summer	2 ft.	white, pink, deep reds
Phlox	summer	1-1/2 ft.	very wide range except orange and blue
Poppy*	winter	2 ft.	white, yellow, pink, orange, red
Snapdragon	autumn	2 ft.	white, yellow through red
Sweet Alyssum	all year	1 ft.	white through purple
Sweet Pea	spring	2 ft.	white through purple, pink
Zinnia	summer	2-1/2 ft.	yellow through orange and red

*Perennial varieties available

FLOWERING PERENNIALS			
COMMON NAME	TIME OF BLOOM	MAXIMUM HEIGHT	COLORS
Aster	summer — autumn	2 to 3 ft.	wide range: blue, pink, yellow, white
Bleeding Heart	spring — summer	2 ft.	pinkish blooms
Chrysanthemum	summer — autumn	2 to 3 ft.	wide range: white, pink, yellow, rust
Columbine	summer	3 to 4 ft.	range from pink to purple
Crocus*	spring	6 in.	white, yellow, pink, blue
Daffodil*	spring	1 to 2 ft.	primarily yellow
Dahlia	autumn	3 ft.	pink, red, yellow
Geranium	summer	1 ft.	pink through blue
Gladiolus*	spring — autumn	2 to 3 ft.	white, yellow through red
Hyacinth*	spring	1 ft.	white through purple
Iris*	spring — summer	2 to 3 ft.	white, yellow, purple
Narcissus*	spring	2 ft.	white through yellow
Peony	spring	2 ft.	white, pink, purple
Periwinkle	spring	low, trailing	white through purple
Primrose	spring — summer	1-1/2 ft.	white, yellow through purple
Rose	spring — autumn	3 to 4 ft.	white, yellow through red
Tulip*	spring	2-1/2 ft.	white, yellow through red

*Planted as bulbs

PLANTING GARDENS

▶ Preparing the Site

Preparing a site for a garden bed is the same as preparing a site for lawns, Page 26. If the area is small or you are working around existing plants, use a spade for tilling the soil. Be careful not to disturb the root systems of the existing plants.

Fertilizer requirements for garden plants are different than for lawns. For garden plants, use a fertilizer high in phosphorus, such as 5-10-10. The second number in the formula 5-10-10 is the percentage of phosphorus in the product. Usually, the directions on the package will specify how much fertilizer to use.

If the planned garden is next to the lawn, lay an edging board or mowing strip to separate the garden from the lawn area. Be sure to lay the board or mowing strip before planting.

▶ Methods of Planting

There are basically two ways of planting a garden: Planting seeds or bulbs and transplanting nursery stock.

Many annuals and perennials can be planted from seed. The advantages in planting from seed are:

- Plants do not suffer transplant "shock".
- Seeds are inexpensive.
- More varieties of plants are available.

There are many new and convenient forms in which to buy seeds:

- Seed tapes with seeds properly spaced along a tape which dissolves in the soil.
- Rolls impregnated with seeds that are unrolled on prepared soil.
- Peat pots you fill with potting soil and plant with a seed. When the plants are large enough, the whole pot is planted.
- Seeds with a coating on them to indicate flower color and make them easier to handle.

Whatever form you use, be sure to follow the directions on the package.

Methods of Planting

Annuals and perennials are available as nursery stock in trays or pots.

The advantage of transplanting nursery stock is that you do not have to wait several weeks to have something green growing in the ground.

When selecting annuals and perennials from nursery stock, look for:

- Small and compact plants, rather than leggy plants.
- Plants that are not in bloom. They will last longer.
- Plants with good green color with no yellowing or browning at the edges of leaves.

Evergreen and flowering shrubs are usually available as nursery stock.

If you are planting a mixed garden, mark out the areas for each type of plant on the prepared soil. Markings can be "drawn" on the soil with a stick, outlined with stakes and strings or curves made with lengths of rope.

Make a corresponding sketch on paper and label each area with the plant names to use as a reference when planting.

If planting nursery stock, go to Page 82.

If planting bulbs, go to Page 82.

If planting seeds, continue.

▶ Planting Seeds

Be sure it is the right time of year to plant your seeds. Directions are on the seed package. Seeds planted too early will not germinate in cool soil. Those planted too late will not complete their growth cycle.

Soil should be moist but not wet when planting.

A disease which prevents germination of newly planted seeds is called "damping off". To assure success for your planting, treat seeds with a chemical to prevent "damping off". The seeds are mixed with a chemical which coats the seed. Directions are on the package.

If seeds are too small to handle easily, mix them with several times their bulk of fine sand in the package or a salt shaker.

Planting Seeds

Seeds can be planted in rows or broadcast over an area.

If broadcasting seeds, scatter the seed or seed and sand mixture over the desired area. Cover the seeded area with fine soil, sawdust or peat moss according to the depth recommended on the seed package. Then go to Step 6.

If planting in rows, continue.

When planting seeds in rows, mark rows in a north-south direction, if possible. This allows sunlight to reach both sides of the plants. Use a board as a guide to make straight furrows. The board can be used to stand on when planting the seeds.

For shallow furrows, use a hoe or rake handle, or your hands. For deeper furrows, use the corner of a hoe blade.

1. Make a furrow [1] the depth and distance apart recommended on the seed package.

2. If using seed and sand mixture, gently tap out the mixture [2] along the furrow.

3. If using seed alone, drop the seeds [3] one at a time into the furrow. Follow the spacing recommended on the seed package.

4. Using the back of a hoe or your hands, gently fill in the furrow [4].

Planting Seeds

5. Sprinkle a thin layer of fine soil, sawdust or peat moss over the seeded area.

Using sawdust or peat moss prevents the soil from crusting over and allows the germinating seeds to break through the surface easily.

6. Press the soil [1] over the seeds to assure that it makes contact with the seeds. Use the back of a hoe or your hands.

7. Using a watering can or a hose with a fine-mist sprayer nozzle, water thoroughly. To prevent washing the seeds away, apply a small amount of water. Let it soak in and repeat watering

If snails and slugs are a problem in your area, place bait around the newly seeded area. Follow package directions and cautions carefully.

When seedings show two pair of leaves [2], thin to the recommended distance.

The soil must be kept moist until the seeds germinate. Follow the procedures described for watering newly seeded lawns, Page 33.

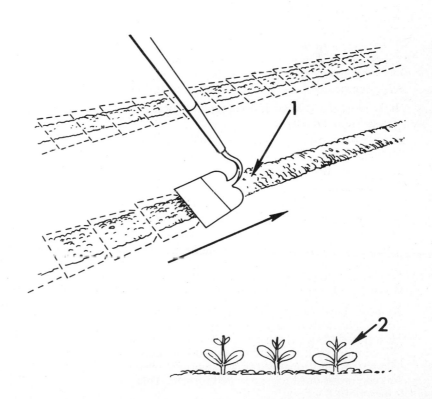

PLANTING A GARDEN

▶ Planting Nursery Stock

Nursery stock is purchased as bare root plants in a state of dormancy, or as living plants growing in groups in flats or trays or growing individually in pots or cans.

If the plant has damaged stems or branches, the damaged parts should be cut off and removed.

Commercially available sprays may be applied to the foliage of newly transplanted plants to control moisture loss. Follow directions on the label.

Rooting hormones and vitamins may be used to help the root system get established quickly.

If planting bare root plants, follow the procedure described on Page 62. Be sure to follow watering instructions for the new plants.

If planting from flats, trays, pots or cans, follow the procedure described on Page 52. Be sure to follow watering instructions for the new plants. If snails or slugs are a problem in your area, place bait around the newly planted area. Follow package directions and cautions carefully.

▶ Planting Bulbs

Be sure to plant bulbs at the right time of year. Time to plant is usually printed on the package. The recommended spacing between bulbs is also given on the package.

Flowers from bulbs generally look best when planted in an area that will hold at least 6 to 10 bulbs. They will produce more bulbs with each growing season.

A bulb is generally planted at a depth twice its height. A 2-inch bulb is planted 4 inches deep. There are exceptions to this, but planting depth is usually given on the package.

Bulbs are classified as Hardy or Tender. Tender bulbs may not survive winter conditions and must be removed from the soil during winter or completely covered with a 3-inch mulch of leaves, peat moss or evergreen boughs for protection. This mulch should be removed in the spring before shoots reach 2 inches above the soil level.

Planting Bulbs

1. Using a trowel or spade, dig an area [1] large enough to hold all the bulbs at the proper spacing and at the proper depth.

If planting many large bulbs, a separate hole may be made for each bulb.

If bulb has loose, leafy tip, tip should be toward top of the hole. The package shows proper planting position of the bulbs.

2. Place bulb in hole. Press bulb in firm contact with the soil at the bottom of the hole to make sure there is no air under the bulb.

When hole is filled, the bulb should be completely covered with soil and there should be a saucer-shaped depression [2] to hold moisture. Water thoroughly.

In most areas, the normal rainfall will provide sufficient moisture after the initial watering. However, additional watering will be required in dry climates or if the normal rainfall is reduced. When such additional watering is required, water to keep moist until roots are well formed. This takes about 8 weeks.

▶ **General Maintenance**

General maintenance of the established garden is the same as for ground cover. The information in the Ground Cover section, beginning on Page 55, includes procedures for:

> Watering
> Fertilizing
> Trimming
> Controlling Insects, Diseases
> and Weeds

For pruning and trimming shrubs and taller perennial plants, use the procedures for trees and shrubs, Page 69.

Tip pinching [1] will help some annual flowers and low-growing plants to spread and produce more flowers. Wait until the annuals are 5 to 8 inches tall or the first flower bud forms before tip pinching.

You can encourage annuals to bloom longer by removing faded flowers before they go to seed. Use a scissors or pruning tool. Do not trim faded flowers if you want plants to reseed themselves.

General Maintenance

During the blossoming period, much of the plant vitality is used for producing the blossoms. Removing some flower buds [1] before they blossom will help the remaining buds develop into larger and healthier flowers.

If you do not want perennial plants to produce seeds, remove spent blossoms. This will direct plant energy to general plant growth.

Some very tall annuals and perennials benefit from staking for support. Insert the stake [2] in the ground a few inches from the stem. Tie a loop around the stake first. Then tie a loop around the plant stem. This will make a figure-eight pattern.

Leave fading foliage on bulbs until it turns brown. The leaves manufacture the nutrients needed for the following year's bloom.

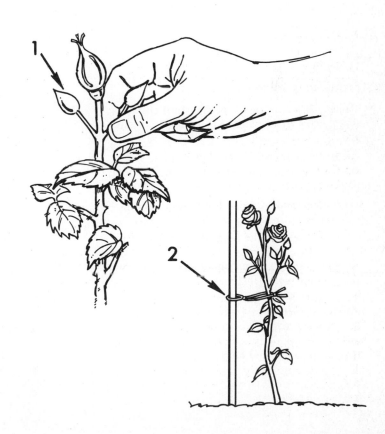

▶ Propagating Plants

Plants that develop thick crowns of roots and stems or those that develop bulb or tuberous root systems benefit by dividing every two to three years.

Dividing gives you new plants and gives the plants needed room for healthy growth.

Plants that bloom in the spring should be divided in the early fall. Divide fall-blooming plants in the spring before they start vigorous growth.

1. Using garden fork, remove plant or clump of plants [1] from the soil.

2. Shake the soil from the root system.

3. If the plant has bulbs or a tuberous root system, cut [2] or pull the bulbs or tubers apart. If tubers have an eye near the stem of the plant, be sure it is included in the cut-off section.

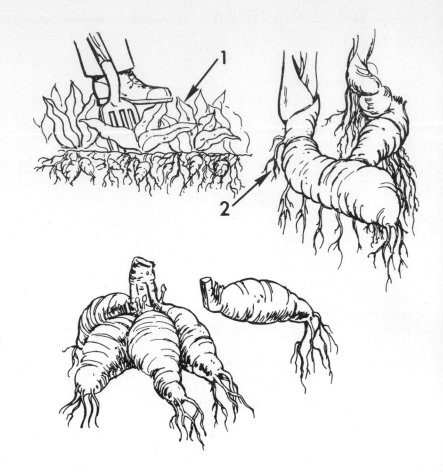

Propagating Plants

If plants are clumped together, pull clump apart into several plants [1] of approximately the same size.

The outer parts are more vigorous and will survive transplanting better than the tougher, center portion.

Very tough roots and stems of some plants can be cut with a knife or spade.

4. Place one of the separated plants back into the soil from which it was removed [2]. Press soil in firm contact with root system.

Plants should be transplanted as soon as possible to prevent excessive moisture loss. The exposed roots must not be allowed to dry. Bulbs and tubers may be allowed to dry out, stored and replanted later.

AREA FERTILIZED	DATE	TYPE OF FERTILIZER
AREA FERTILIZED	DATE	TYPE OF FERTILIZER

AREA FERTILIZED	DATE	TYPE OF FERTILIZER

AREA FERTILIZED	DATE	TYPE OF FERTILIZER

| AREA FERTILIZED | DATE | TYPE OF FERTILIZER |

AREA FERTILIZED	DATE	TYPE OF FERTILIZER
AREA FERTILIZED	DATE	TYPE OF FERTILIZER

TYPE OF PLANT	DATE	PURCHASED AT
TYPE OF PLANT	DATE	PURCHASED AT

TYPE OF PLANT	DATE	PURCHASED AT

TYPE OF PLANT	DATE	PURCHASED AT

TYPE OF PLANT	DATE	PURCHASED AT

TYPE OF PLANT	DATE	PURCHASED AT

TYPE OF PLANT	DATE	PURCHASED AT

| TYPE OF PLANT | DATE | PURCHASED AT |

TYPE OF PLANT	DATE	PURCHASED AT

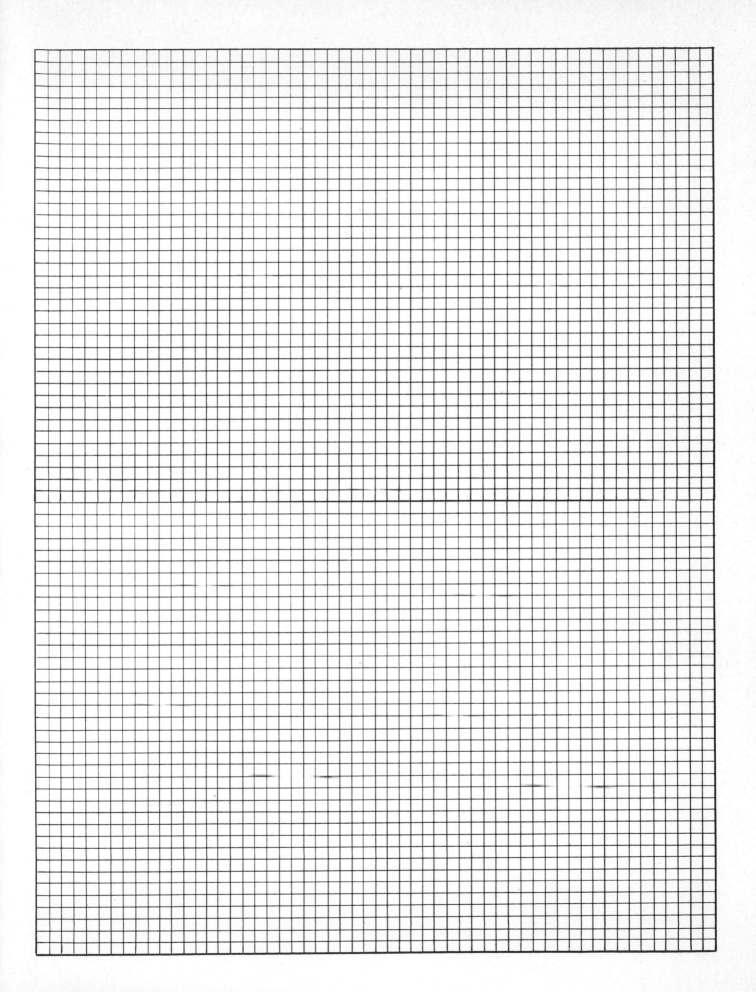

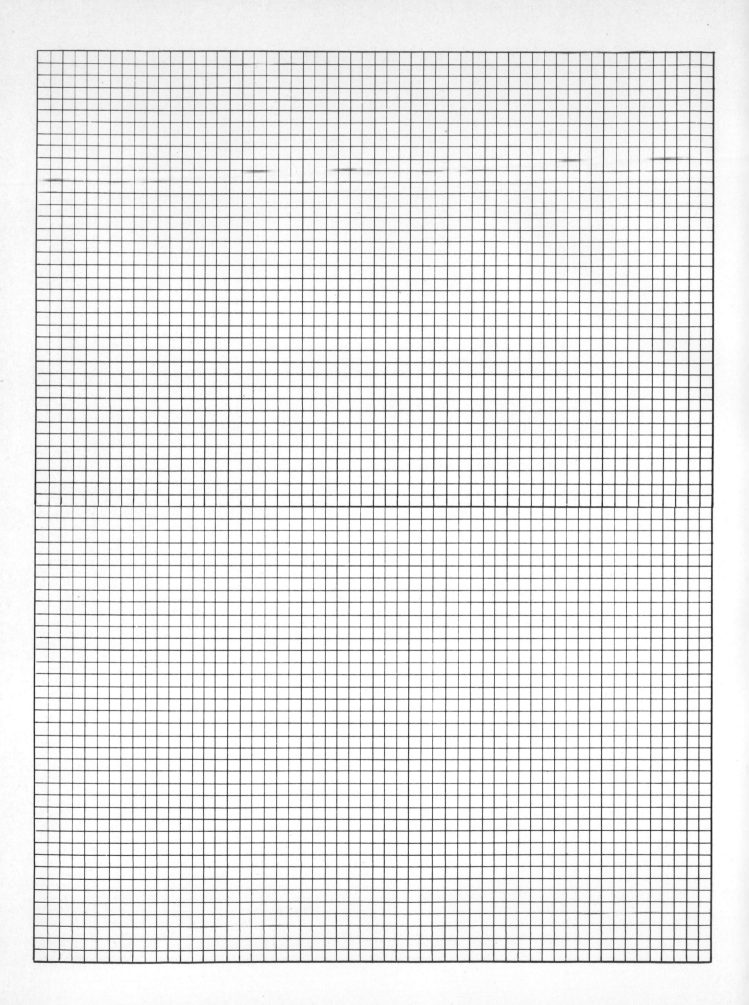

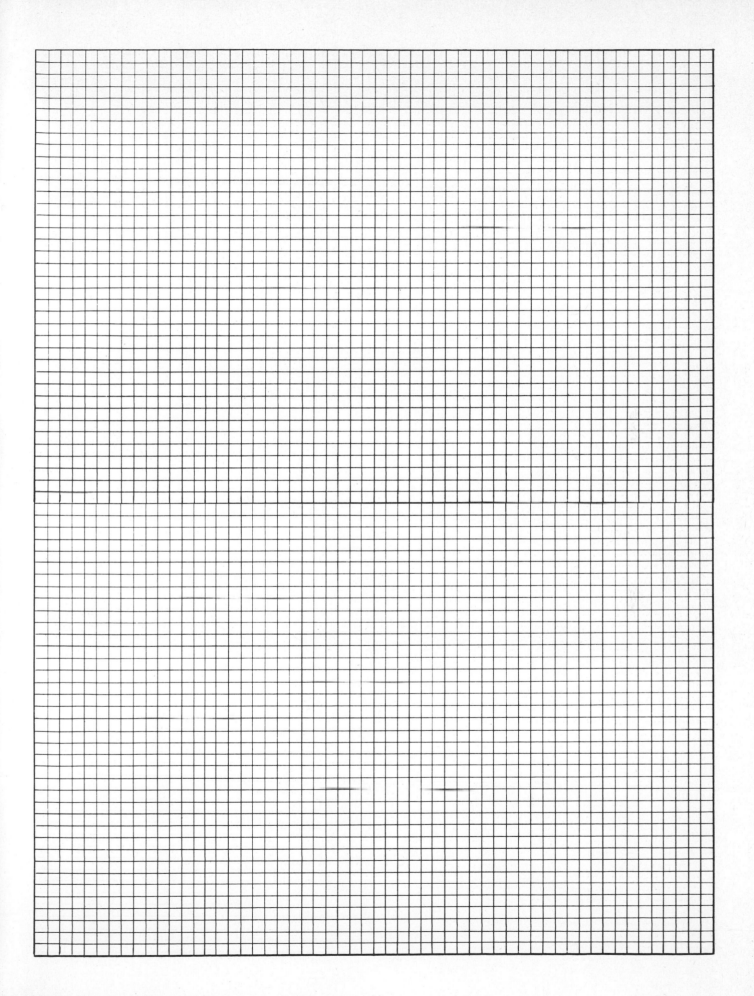

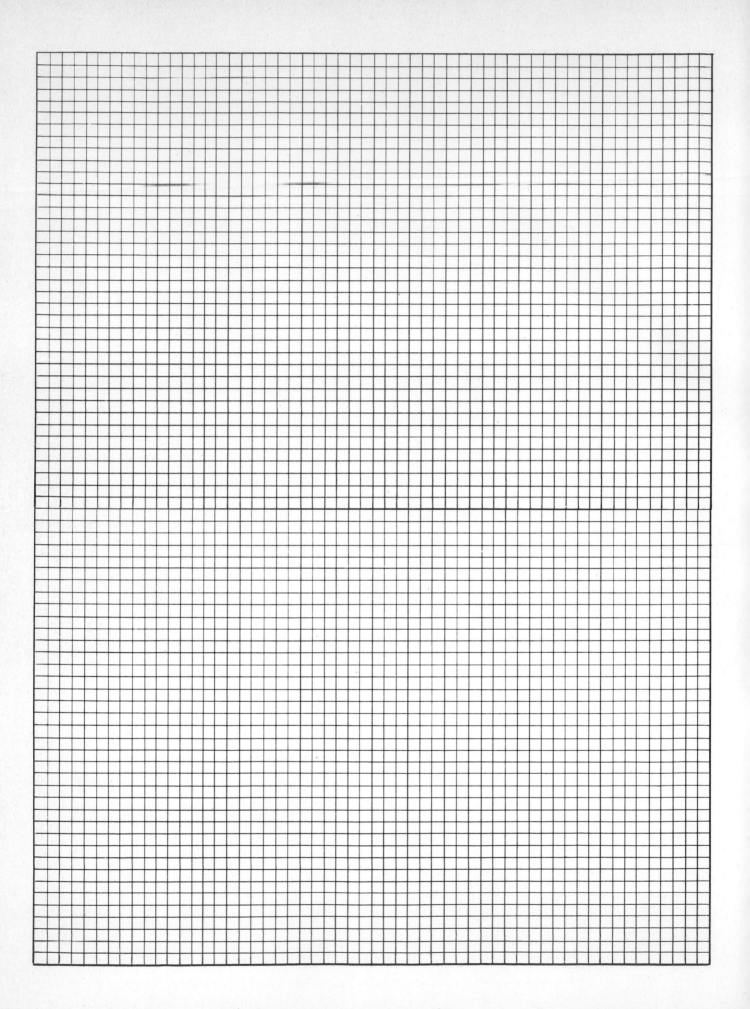

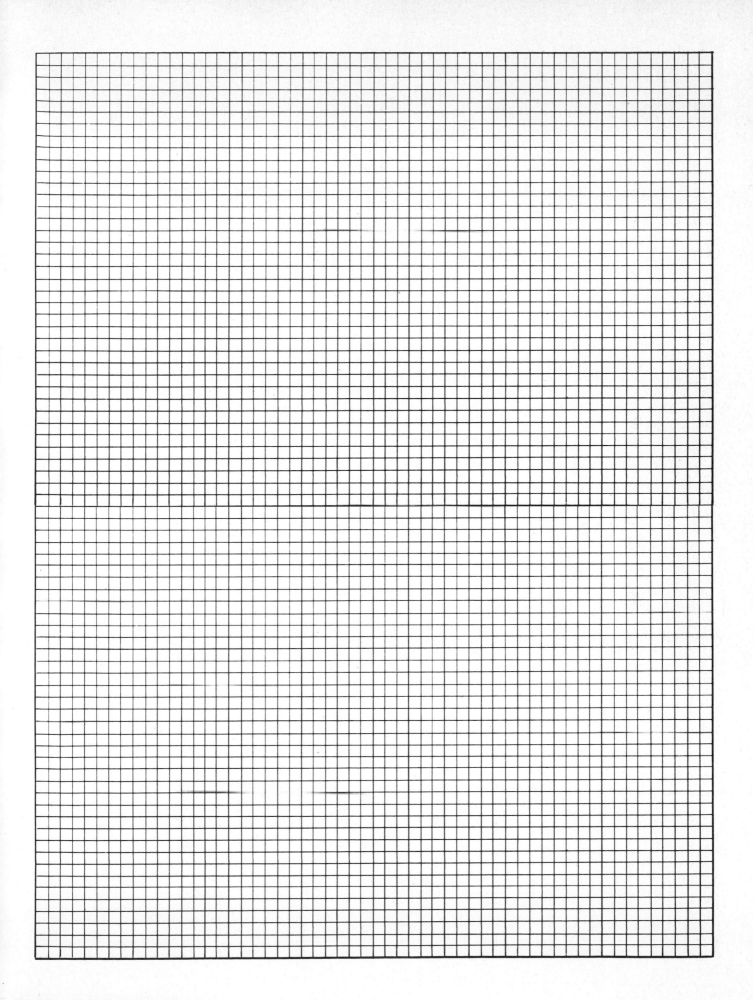

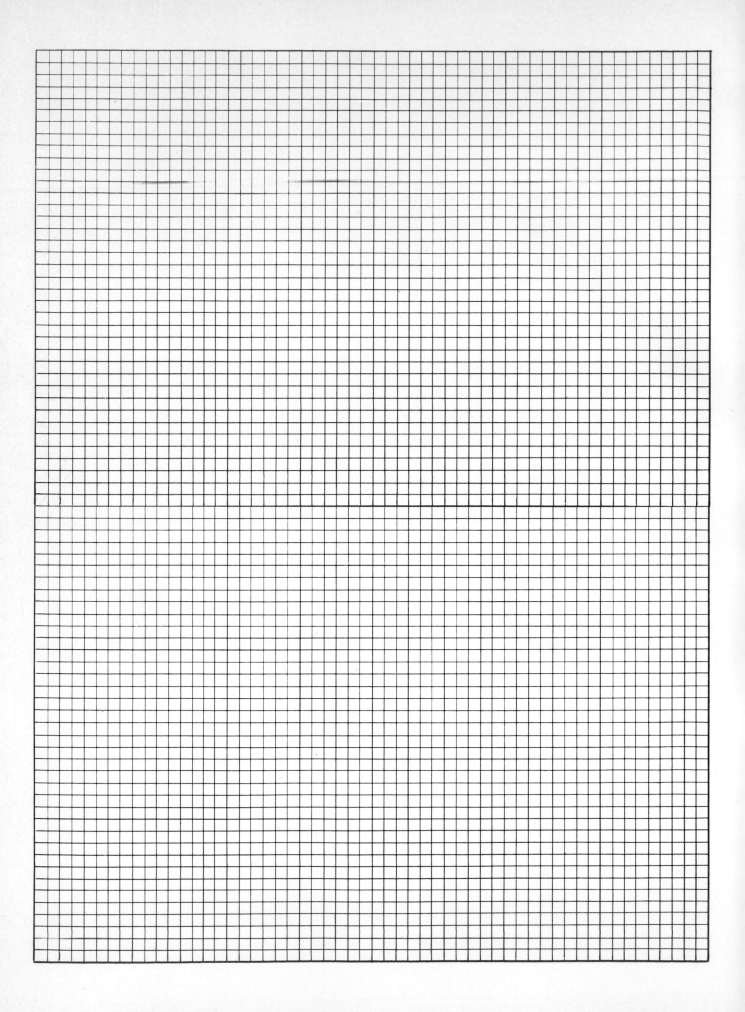

NOTES

NOTES